Sacred Highlands and Islands

SACRED PLACES SERIES

Sacred Highlands and Islands

SCOTLAND'S CHURCHES SCHEME

SAINT ANDREW PRESS
Edinburgh

First published in 2011 by
SAINT ANDREW PRESS
121 George Street
Edinburgh EH2 4YN

The cover photograph is of St Andrew's, Tongue. © A. Stewart Brown

Copyright text and maps © Scotland's Churches Scheme, 2011
Copyright *Invitation to Pilgrimage* article © Alexander Gordon, 2011
Copyright *Sacred Highlands and Islands* article © John Hume, 2011
Colour photographs in this book are copyright and are used with permission.
Raymond Parks: 21, 101, 136; A. Stewart Brown: 25, 33, 40, 65, 66, 72;
Simpson & Brown: 28. All other images by SCS member churches.

ISBN 978 0 7152 0955 4

British Library Cataloguing in Publication Data
A catalogue record for this book is available from the British Library.

It is the publisher's policy to only use papers that are natural and recyclable and that
have been manufactured from timber grown in renewable, properly managed forests.
All of the manufacturing processes of the papers are expected to conform to the
environmental regulations of the country of origin.

Typeset in Enigma by Waverley Typesetters, Warham, Norfolk
Manufactured in Great Britain by Bell & Bain Ltd, Glasgow

BUCKINGHAM PALACE

As Patron of Scotland's Churches Scheme, I warmly welcome this publication as part of the *Sacred Places* series of books being produced by the Scheme.

The story of the heritage and culture of Scotland would be lacking significantly without a strong focus on its churches and sacred sites. I am sure that this guidebook will be a source of information and enjoyment both to the people of Scotland and to our visitors.

Anne

Scotland's Churches Scheme

www.sacredscotland.org.uk

Scotland's Churches Scheme is an ecumenical charitable trust, providing an opportunity to access the nation's living heritage of faith by assisting the 'living' churches in membership to:

- Promote spiritual understanding by enabling the public to appreciate all buildings designed for worship and active as living churches
- Work together with others to make the Church the focus of the community
- Open their doors with a welcoming presence
- Tell the story of the building (however old or new), its purpose and heritage (artistic, architectural and historical)
- Provide information for visitors, young and old

The Scheme has grown rapidly since its inception in 1994, and there are now more than 1,200 churches in membership. These churches are to be found across all parts of Scotland and within all the denominations.

The *Sacred Scotland* theme promoted by Scotland's Churches Scheme focuses on the wish of both visitors and local communities to be able to access our wonderful range of church buildings in a meaningful way, whether the visit be occasioned by spiritual or heritage motivation or both. The Scheme can advise and assist member churches on visitor welcome, and, with its range of 'how-to' brochures, provide information on research, presentation, security and other live issues relating to the buildings and associated graveyards. With its network of local representatives, the Scheme encourages the opening of doors and the care of tourists and locals alike, and offers specific services such as the provision of grants for organ-playing.

Sacred Scotland (www.sacredscotland.org.uk), the website of Scotland's Churches Scheme, opens the door to Scotland's story by exploring living traditions of faith in city, town, village and island across the country. The site is a portal to access information on Scotland's churches of all denominations and is a starting point for your special journeys.

The Scheme has also embarked, with support from Scottish Enterprise and Historic Scotland, on the identification and promotion of Scotland's Pilgrim Ways, with the huge resource of its expanding website and database of sacred sites. With the growing awareness and enthusiasm for such an initiative, a pilot project is already under way and is seen as a welcome development of the Scheme's existing activity and publications.

We are delighted to be working with Saint Andrew Press in the publication of this *Sacred Places* series of regional guides to Scotland's churches. In 2009, the first three volumes were published – *Sacred South-West Scotland*; *Sacred Edinburgh and Midlothian*; and *Sacred Fife and the Forth Valley*. In 2010, a further three volumes were published – *Sacred Borders and East Lothian*; *Sacred Glasgow and the Clyde Valley*; and *Sacred North-East Scotland*. This volume, *Sacred Highlands and Islands*, is one of the final three to be published in 2011, now covering the whole country. The others are *Sacred Argyll and Clyde* and *Sacred Perthshire and the Tay Valley*. We are grateful to the authors of the introductory articles, Professor John Hume, one of our trustees, and Alex Gordon, for their expert contributions to our understanding of sacred places.

The growth of 'spiritual tourism' worldwide is reflected in the million-plus people who visit Scotland's religious sites annually. We hope that the information in this book will be useful in bringing alive the heritage as well as the ministry of welcome which our churches offer. In the words of our former President, Lady Marion Fraser: 'we all owe a deep debt of gratitude to the many people of vision who work hard and imaginatively to create a lasting and peaceful atmosphere which you will carry away with you as a special memory when you leave'.

DR BRIAN FRASER
Director, Scotland's Churches Scheme
Dunedin, Holehouse Road, Eaglesham, Glasgow G76 0JF

Scotland's Churches Scheme: local representatives

Rev. Willis Jones (*Central Highland*)   Mr Robert Cormack (*Orkney*)
Rev. Alan Lamb (*West Highland*)   Rev. David Cooper (*Shetland*)
Ms Esme Duncan (*North Highland*)   Fr Michael McDonald (*Western Isles*)

Invitation to Pilgrimage
Highlands and Islands

Why pilgrimage?

From the very earliest moments of recorded religious history, experiences of God have been frequently afforded to people on the move. The formative experience of the people of Israel was the forty years of pilgrimage from a life of slavery in Egypt to a new life in the land of promise, and this was a time when the people discovered themselves and the reality of the God who called them into being. As time went by, life itself began to be seen as a journey, a pilgrimage of discovery. To focus the attention, many religious traditions have intense periods of pilgrimage to be undertaken at specific moments during life. In the Christian tradition, the earliest pilgrimages were made to sites in the Holy Land which were specifically associated with Jesus' life and ministry – but there was rather more to pilgrimage than just the desire to see where it was that Jesus had lived.

Sacred places were seen to be special, where the veil between heaven and earth was very thin. So, in the early Christian centuries, more and more places of pilgrimage were identified – such as the place of the martyrdom of St Peter and of St Paul in Rome. Not everyone, however, had the means or the leisure to take part in lengthy pilgrimages to far-off places, and soon other sites were identified as holy by the association with someone recognised as a saint, or marked by some other sacred phenomenon. In the Celtic Church, with its close relationship with the natural world, pilgrimage was very popular and would often be associated with symbolic actions such as drinking water from a holy well, the placing of parts of one's body on a sacred stone, and the leaving of an offering such as a strip of cloth tied to a thorn bush, or a coin embedded in a tree trunk. This devotional exercise became known as 'making a pilgrimage' and was seen as a specially intense period of prayer – as an act of penance for sin, petition for a personal blessing or for a friend or relative in particular need. Whereas that might provide the religious rationale for a pilgrimage, inevitably there were plenty of other more mundane ones – and the incidental values of exploration, of the dispelling of past prejudices, and of the profound nourishment achieved through an encounter with the roots of our faith and the histories of those who have gone before us, are of significant value today as always.

Although the area covered in this book is now one characterised by space and lack of population, it was not always such, and there is evidence of much larger numbers of people living in the Highlands and Islands from very early times, though in terrain which has always been rugged and exposed to the wild elements of wind, sea and weather. So, you will find many pre-Christian sites in the Highlands which have a degree of sacredness about them. The most accessible are in the care of Historic Scotland. They include the burial cairns and standing stones at Clava, near Inverness, the enormous Camster Cairns and the Hill o' Many Stanes in Caithness. Although it is sometimes disputed, the first Christian missionary to reach the Highlands was almost certainly St Ninian, who came from Whithorn to Glenurquhart. Near Drumnadrochit, at Temple Pier, are the remains of St Ninian's Cell; and in St Ninian's Scottish Episcopal Church in Glenurquhart is a stone on which he is reputed to have stood to preach. A little later came St Columba, whose missionary journeys from the island of Iona included visits to Ardnamurchan and to Inverness, where he is said to have preached on the hill where the present Old High Church is situated. His visit to the Pictish King Brude resulted in the conversion of the king, whose stronghold is supposed to have been Craig Phadraig, Inverness; and a modern pilgrimage to this point has been revived.

A contemporary of St Columba was St Donnan ('the red-haired martyr'). Although he had wished to become an associate of Columba, the latter rebuffed him. Mortified, Donnan continued to evangelise mainland Scotland. He built a number of chapels, and some extensive monastic buildings at Kildonan in Sutherland, on a par with Candida Casa built by St Ninian at Whithorn. His cell was near the Helmsdale river; and parts of the rock from which he preached to people on the other side, when the river was too high, remain visible today.

To discover some of the riches of the late Celtic Church, a visit to Portmahomack is a must. The former Tarbat Parish Church been converted into the Tarbat Discovery Centre (www.tarbatdiscovery.co.uk) and contains material relating to recent excavations and to Pictish carved stones in the area. It would appear that, between the eighth and eleventh centuries, there was much religious activity here. A little further south, on the Black Isle, there is a lot of evidence of Christian activity from the eighth century onwards, and there are more interesting stones in the Groam House Museum at Rosemarkie (www.groamhouse.org.uk). Fortrose was an important Christian centre, and parts of its later Cathedral still remain.

There are many smaller sites of interest in the discovery of religious roots, and a good number of holy wells to be found in the Highlands, including 'clootie wells' renowned for the purity and healing power of their waters. The term 'clootie' refers to the practice of tying strips of cloth, as offerings, to bushes beside these wells (see above). Throughout the Highlands, you will come across this practice even today. St Maelrubha ('the red priest', and an extremely important missionary to the Highlands in the century following St Columba) is associated with one such healing well – the properties of which were said to cure insanity – on a tiny island in Loch Maree where Maelrubha's cell was to be found. His grave is thought to be in Applecross, in the churchyard where he also lived.

Before the Reformation in the Highlands, Tain was one of Britain's great pilgrimage sites – and information about this can be found in the 'Tain through Time' pilgrimage centre (www.tainmuseum.org.uk) in St Duthac's Churchyard. One of the last kings of Scotland, James IV, a man who brought about considerable betterments for his land and people, made numerous pilgrimages to Tain in the fifteenth and early sixteenth centuries. St Duthac had a reputation as a worker of miracles and a man of great learning in the eleventh century. Born in Tain close to the church that bears his name, he died in Armagh, and his remains were translated to Tain in the thirteenth century with great rejoicing.

The Western and Northern Isles have a special place in the religious history of Scotland, as they provided places of refuge and security, or staging posts for missionaries from further afield approaching mainland Scotland. In this volume, you will find mention of many of these places and their stories – and no pilgrimage to the sacred places can be complete without crossing the waters surrounding our shores. On the islands, you will discover a quite unique experience both of life and of religious faith, both past and present.

At the time of the Reformation, many of the holy places in the Highlands, including the pilgrimage sites, were attacked by zealous reformers, and there were attempts to forbid any of the practices previously associated with them, under pain of severe ecclesiastical sanction. Nevertheless, while much was lost at that time, it is still possible to discover something of our religious heritage from those earlier days, nestling in the Highlands, and its places made holy by our fathers in faith, who lived, taught, prayed and worked, and brought much blessing to our land. The Reformation heritage has produced its own places of pilgrimage, too, and is shown in a whole new tradition of church-building, plenty of examples of which may be found across the Highlands and Islands. Some have evocative resonances of fidelity through adversity. For example, the Croick Church at Ardgay has an east window scratched in 1845 by those evicted from Glencalvie during the Highland Clearances. That church, built to a design by Thomas Telford, has furnishings which are virtually unchanged since it was built earlier in the nineteenth century. Because of their relative inaccessibility, the islands have sometimes proved to be places untouched by religious change, as in the case of Barra. However, in the case of Iona there has been in the last century a rediscovery of the riches of an earlier tradition of life in community which nurtured St Columba and his followers.

You will find very much within the covers of this volume which will help you discover more about the ways in which our ancestors practised their faith, understood their lives, and related to God. The places where they did this are well worth exploring. As you do so, may you find joy, nourishment and enrichment, and –

> *God with thee in every pass*
> *Jesus with thee on every knoll*
> *Spirit with thee by water's roll*
> *On headland, on ridge and on grass*
>
> *Each sea and land, each moor and each mead,*
> *Each eve's lying down, each rising's morn*
> *In the wave-trough, or on foam-crest borne*
> *Each step which thy journey doth end.*
>
> *(from a traditional Celtic pilgrim blessing)*

VERY REV. CANON ALEXANDER GORDON
Provost and Rector of St Andrew's Cathedral, Inverness

Introduction

Sacred Highlands and Islands

One cannot understand the different cultures of the Highlands and Islands, in all their variety and richness, without trying to disentangle some of the strands of belief in the 'sacred' which underpin those cultures. This Introduction is essentially about places and buildings associated with religious observance, but it would be fair to say that in the Highlands and Islands one is never separated very far from a sense of the spiritual. In that context, reference will be made to churches which have become ruinous, or are no longer used for their original purpose, if they are of significant historical, architectural and spiritual interest. The treatment is explicitly not architectural-historical, as there are excellent architectural guides already available.

The Highlands is a term used to define that part of Scotland north and west of the so-called 'highland boundary fault' which separates the older rocks of the area from the younger rocks of the central Lowlands in which most of Scotland's people live. It is usual to exclude the north-east of Scotland – the old counties of Kincardineshire, Aberdeenshire, Banffshire and Moray – from the geological Highlands, and, for administrative reasons, Argyll and Bute, including the most of the islands known as the Inner Hebrides. The Isle of Skye, now linked to mainland Scotland by a bridge, is administratively part of the Highlands, as is its neighbour Raasay. The other island groups in our area have since 1975 been administered by separate local authorities, though the Western Isles were before that time divided

Fig. 1. Lunna Kirk, Shetland

Fig. 2. Nesting Parish Church, Shetland

between the old counties of Ross and Cromarty and Inverness-shire. The Northern Isles – Orkney and Shetland – have long had their own local authorities. All three island groups were under Norse control for centuries, in the cases of Orkney and Shetland until the fifteenth century, and they have distinctive characters. Orkney and Caithness have some characteristics in common, but Shetland and the Western Isles are without parallel. Their distance from the mainland has resulted in the development of distinctive cultures. All three island groups deserve separate consideration from the Highlands, and are discussed individually below.

Shetland

The Shetland Isles are the island group farthest from the Scottish mainland. Their history and prehistory are linked firmly to their position in relation to what are now the Scandinavian countries. The archipelago seems to have, however, lacked the mystical meaning to early settlers that Orkney possessed. The fish in its waters were an important source of wealth, as was the sheltered harbour of Lerwick, which became a significant trading centre. There is little surviving physical evidence of prehistoric religion in the islands, or of the medieval Church. There may be medieval fabric in the little Lunna Kirk (Fig. 1), with its curious buttresses, but this dates for the most part from 1753, and is therefore part of the oldest group of churches, which date from the eighteenth century – simple Georgian buildings like the parish churches of Tingwall (1788-90, **7**), Fetlar (1790, **12**) and Nesting (1782-93, Fig. 2). Lunna and Tingwall both have fine canopied pulpits. Bressay (1812, **9**) is comparable. Sandwick (1807, Fig. 3), though larger, must have originally been in a similar style, but was altered in 1897. St John's, Baltasound, Unst (1825-7, **13**) was originally a simple Georgian church, but had a unique concrete tower added in 1959.

The increasing prosperity of Lerwick, based on fishing,

Fig. 3. Sandwick Parish Church, Shetland

encouraged the construction of a new parish church (St Columba's) in 1828 (**1**) in a simple classical style. It was probably the success of fishing that resulted in the construction of two churches in Yell in 1832 – St John's, Mid Yell (**18**) and St Olaf's, Cullivoe (**19**). The latter has an unusual castellated frontage. Scalloway, Shetland's second-largest settlement, built a new pier in 1830, and in 1840–1 a new church was built (**6**). The Disruption in 1843 did not affect Shetland as much as the Western Isles and the Highlands, but in 1843 two very distinctive Free churches with very low-pitched roofs were built on Unst. One, at Baliasta, is now roofless; the other, at Uyeasound (**15**), is now the parish church for the island. Weisdale (1863, **8**) was also built as a Free church.

Both Methodism and Congregationalism became (and remain) popular in Shetland. Scalloway Methodist Church (1861, Fig. 4) is a simple building, but the Adam Clarke Memorial Methodist Church in Lerwick (1872, **4**) is in Gothic Revival style, relatively rare in Shetland. East Yell (1892, **20**) and Haroldswick, Unst (1993, **14**) Methodist churches testify to the continuing vitality of the denomination. There are two Scottish Episcopal churches in Shetland. St Magnus, Lerwick (1862–4, **2**), a simple Gothic Revival building, gained its striking tower in 1891. St Colman's, Yell (1900, **16**) is an unexpected Arts and Crafts Gothic building in such a remote place. The success of the herring-fishing industry in the later nineteenth and early twentieth century made Shetland reasonably prosperous, and other churches built in that period included Gulberwick (1898, **5**), Bigton (1905, Fig. 5) and Shetland's only Roman Catholic church, St Margaret's, Lerwick (1911, **3**).

There are many other church buildings in Shetland, but rural depopulation has resulted in the closure of a number of them; and a number of others have been converted into houses or otherwise adapted. Most rural Shetland churches are simple structures, for instance Ollaberry (1865, Fig. 6), built as a mission church. Many of them are in fine landscape settings and are well worth seeking out.

Orkney

Maps of Scotland frequently omit the Northern Isles or relegate them to an inset, reflecting their remoteness from the landmass of the mainland. A map of north-

Fig. 4. Scalloway Methodist Church, Shetland

Fig. 5. Bigton Church of Scotland,
Dunrossness Parish, Shetland

western Europe, however, shows what a pivotal place Orkney is. When you are in Orkney, you are very conscious that it is in a real sense central, with the Scandinavian countries near-neighbours to the east, and the Faeroe Islands, Iceland, Greenland and Canada across unobstructed ocean to the north and west. That the islands were considered particularly sacred in pre-Christian times is amply demonstrated by their unparalleled prehistoric monuments: the Ring of Brodgar, Stones of Stenness, Maes Howe (among other chambered tombs) and the recently discovered great 'temple' at Stenness. This group of monuments in central Orkney still has a powerful sense of the 'other', of a real spirituality.

The scale of these monuments, and their sophistication, strongly suggests their construction by a comparatively settled, agricultural society, which also used the sea as a source of food. Their settlements, of which Skara Brae is only one example, show their ability to live communal but private lives – a form of cooperation which would be necessary to construct the large-scale monuments mentioned above.

There is evidence of Norse Christianity in the great cathedral of St Magnus (founded 1137, **21**), Kirkwall, and also in the ruined churches of St Magnus, Egilsay (probably c. 1135–8, Fig. 7), and the round church of St Nicholas, Orphir (early twelfth century, Fig. 8). Parts of St Magnus, Birsay (c. 1060 on, **25**) are also probably from the Norse period, as are St Boniface, Papa Westray (twelfth century, **35)** and the little ruined chapel on the island of Eynhallow.

Of particular interest are the remains of the church on the Brough of Birsay, a cathedral which preceded Kirkwall. The plan of this little building, with nave, chancel and semi-circular apse, is very similar to those of Leuchars (Fife) and Dalmeny (Edinburgh), and can be seen paralleled in churches throughout the western seaboard of

Fig. 6. Ollaberry Church of Scotland, Shetland

northern Europe. These are all areas of Norse influence, and the layout of these churches suggests their use for a form of worship specifically Norse in origin. Of the medieval period after the end of Norse rule, a few examples survive, but none in use (apart from St Magnus Cathedral, Kirkwall, not completed until about 1500).

The prosperity of Orkney agriculture from the late eighteenth century resulted in displacement of older communities and the construction of new churches. At first these were small, simple structures, such as Old St Mary's, Burwick (1790, **36**) and St Peter's, Eastside (1801, **37**), both on South Ronaldsay, and the old church on North Ronaldsay (1812, Fig. 9), subsequently dignified by the addition of a tower in 1906. The nearly contemporary East Mainland Parish Church at Holm (1814, **26**) is unusual in having been built as a Secession (Antiburgher) church. The construction of simple, 'vernacular' churches continued until the mid-nineteenth century. Good examples are St Columba's, Longhope, on Hoy (1832, **30**); St Michael's, Harray, Mainland (1836, **27**); and St Peter's, Sandwick (1836 and later, **28**). St Ann's, Papa Westray (1841, **34**) is a very late example of this type of building. St Margaret's, St Margaret's Hope, South Ronaldsay (1856, 1870, **38**) is simple but more urban in style. The enormous Romanesque former East Church, Kirkwall (1847) was built for the United Presbyterian Church; it is now council offices. As in Shetland, the Disruption of 1843 had little effect.

There are no large Gothic Revival churches in Orkney, apart from the now secularised church of Twatt, Mainland (1874). The largest in use is the present Kirkwall East Church (1892, **22**), originally Kirkwall Baptist. St Olaf's Scottish Episcopal Church (1876, **23**) and the Roman Catholic Church of Our Lady and St Joseph (1877, **24**), both in Kirkwall, are modest Gothic structures, as is St John's, North Walls, a mission church (1883, **31**). St Mary's Scottish Episcopal Church, Stromness (1888, **29**), a very plain building, was also a mission church.

Of all these churches, the cathedral of St Magnus stands out as internationally important. The construction of a great Romanesque church in Orkney, by Norsemen, is continuing evidence of the central spiritual position of Orkney. On a much more modest scale, three little twentieth-century Orkney churches have significance well

Fig. 7. The former St Magnus Church, Egilsay, Orkney

Fig. 8. The former St Magnus Church, Egilsay, Orkney

beyond the islands. Two of these are Arts and Crafts churches. The older is the Chapel of St Colm and St Margaret at Melsetter, Hoy (1900, **32**), a little gem of a building, designed, like the house, by W. R. Lethaby, one of the greatest English Arts and Crafts architects. The other is the Moncur Memorial Church on Stronsay (1955, **39**), the last of Scotland's Arts and Crafts churches, austere but beautiful. These two churches, and indeed all Orkney's other churches, can be fitted into the general history of the Church in Scotland. The last, the Italian Chapel on Lamb Holm (1943–4, **33**), is remarkable not just in Scottish but in world terms. The transformation of a pair of Nissen huts into a moving place for worship by a group of Italian prisoners-of-war engaged in the heavy manual work of constructing the church is, to my mind, further evidence of the continuing spiritual power of Orkney.

The Highlands

The Highlands is large, and varied geologically, topographically, racially and culturally. It is paradoxically united by the difficulties of communication in an area with rugged terrain, bordered by seas which are often hostile. There is only one large urban centre in the Highlands – the city of Inverness – and there are fewer than a dozen sizeable towns. Much of the area is not suited to human habitation, at least in winter, though at one time temporary migration to upland summer pasture was common. Large parts of the interior are now virtually uninhabited. Most communities are, and always have been, small, and often scattered, with houses spread over a wide area. Until about 200 years ago, roads, and wheeled vehicles, were unknown over most of the region, with people reliant on local resources, supplemented by what could be traded by sea or by pack animals.

The most marked character differences within the Highlands

Fig. 9. The former North Ronaldsay Parish Church, Orkney

are between the eastern, relatively dry and fertile districts – Nairnshire, Caithness and the eastern parts of Inverness-shire, Ross and Cromarty and Sutherland – and the centre and west. The wide valleys – straths – penetrating the mountain mass from the east and north have much in common with the eastern coastal strip.

Cultural difference generally reflects topographical and climate variety. In early historic times, the eastern strip was controlled by the northern Picts, though Norse influence was also important. The west was colonised by Gaelic-speaking Celts. In the medieval period, the east was to an increasing extent integrated into the kingdom of Scotland, with the degree of cultural uniformity that this implied. The west was dominated by the semi-independent Lords of the Isles, the difficulties of communication and the warlike character of the Celtic people making control from the Lowlands exceedingly difficult.

The breakdown of the semi-independence of the west began in the eighteenth century, and gained momentum in the nineteenth century. The conclusions of the Jacobite risings of 1715 and 1745–6 were followed by programmes of military road-building which brought increasing Lowland influence to bear on the area, as did the construction of artillery forts and infantry barracks. Lowland influence dramatically increased during the French Revolutionary and Napoleonic wars, when demand for kelp and wool resulted in economic dependence on Lowland markets, internal population movements, and a massive programme of government-assisted road construction. Many Highlanders served in armies overseas. The building of the Caledonian Canal through the Great Glen which separates the northern from the southern Highlands had little economic but great symbolic effect. The development of the steamboat on the Clyde after 1812 had a transforming influence on the western Highlands and Islands; railway-building to the western seaboard from the 1870s to the early 1900s was primarily geared to complement steamer services.

Emigration from the western and northern Highlands was substantial in the nineteenth century. Much of this was voluntary, as employment opportunities and living conditions failed to advance as rapidly in the area as elsewhere. Some of the

Fig. 10. Kilmuir Easter Parish Church, Ross and Cromarty, Highland

Fig. 11. Steeple, Lovat Mausoleum, Wardlaw Parish Church, Kirkhill, Inverness-shire, Highland

population movements within, and out of, the area were forced – the so-called 'Clearances'. The impetus for the Clearances came in part from the landowners' wish initially to introduce kelp-burning and intensive sheep-farming, and later to form sporting estates, and in part from the inability of the land to sustain an increasing population over years of poor harvests. The lack of formal land tenure within the old Celtic-dominated areas made landowner-driven clearance legal – a discriminatory position eventually remedied by the passing of the Crofting Act in 1886, which created secure crofting tenure.

In the eastern and central Highlands, with their drier climate and larger areas of fertile soil, these pressures did not exist to anything like the same extent. The evidence of surviving buildings shows that, at least from the seventeenth century onwards, these areas were much more prosperous, with settlement significantly closer in character to that in the Lowlands. Enclosure and agricultural improvement undoubtedly resulted in people moving off the land, but – as in the Lowlands – this seems to have been a more gradual process, with the general arable-farming use of the land requiring a significantly larger workforce than the sheep-farming introduced in the north and north-west. Fishing, introduced on a commercial scale in the 1780s, was more important and a more reliable source of income than on the north and west coasts, and fishing villages and towns became notably characteristic of the east coast.

Because of the flatter terrain, it was easier to improve communications. The work of the Commissioners for Highland Roads and Bridges, important throughout the Highlands, had a transforming effect in the east, with wheeled vehicles able to

Fig. 12. Boleskine and Abertarff Parish Church, Inverness-shire, Highland

reach the far north by 1820, effectively integrating the area into the rest of Scotland. The building of the Caledonian Canal, at about the same time, also aided this process. The construction of railways in the area from the mid-1850s to the mid-1870s reinforced that process, encouraging the growth of the towns and of some villages. The building of the Dingwall and Skye Railway in the early 1870s brought a large part of the west, and the islands, into the ambit of Inverness and, to a lesser extent, Dingwall. Inverness became the unrivalled capital of the whole of northern Scotland. Railways, too, brought visitors to the area, both tourists anxious to see grand scenery, and rich southerners anxious to display their wealth and status by fishing, stalking and shooting. Much of the upland landmass of the Highlands was divided into sporting estates in the second half of the nineteenth century, resulting in heavy seasonal railway traffic.

Though the middle and upper classes began to forsake the railways for the roads early in the twentieth century, it was not until the 1920s and 1930s that trunk roads were built into the Highlands – first the A9 from Perth to Inverness, and then the A82 from Glasgow to Fort William, and thence up the Great Glen to Inverness. Further significant road improvement did not come until the 1970s. In the 1890s, aluminium-smelting was introduced at Foyers, on Loch Ness, followed by works at Kinlochleven and Fort William, bringing heavy industry to the western Highlands for the first time. In the 1940s and 1950s, hydro-electric power began the modernisation of much of the area; and the opening of an experimental nuclear electric power station at Dounreay, Caithness, in the 1950s brought new life to the far north. The discovery of oil in the North Sea had a more significant impact on the Highlands, with platform construction yards established at Loch Kishorn on the west coast, and on the east at Ardersier near Inverness, and at Nigg, Cromarty. The Cromarty Firth became a base for the maintenance of exploration rigs. An oil terminal was also built at Nigg. These developments and other, smaller ones brought people into the area from the Lowlands and stimulated the growth of the villages along the Cromarty Firth. Since the 1980s, Inverness has grown rapidly, and in 2000 achieved city status. Urban growth has, however, been achieved at the expense of rural depopulation; and large parts of the landward

Fig. 13. Urray Old Parish Church, Ross and Cromarty, Highland

Fig. 14. The former Cromarty Gaelic Church,
Ross and Cromarty, Highland

areas are now very sparsely populated. The area has, however, retained a distinctive character, of which the sacred is still an important part.

The early religious history of the Highlands is obscure, largely because of the paucity of written records. The eastern Highlands and the western areas seem to have had distinctly different experiences of Christianisation, and probably of pre-Christian religion. The bulls and boars of pre-Christian Northern Pictish symbolism possibly hint at some form of animism. The character of the Christian monuments of the northern Picts, and their placing, strongly suggests a prosperous agrarian rather than pastoral society, with landownership established as a concept. Christianisation of this area seems to have been from the culture of the southern Picts. On the west coast, Christian missionaries from Iona (which had strong links with Irish-Celtic Christianity) seem to have been the main influences.

The earliest surviving stone churches in the eastern Highlands are associated with the introduction and development of the feudal system. The establishment of parishes, and of diocesan structures, created fixed gathering points and stipendiary clergy. Cathedrals were built in Fortrose and in Dornoch (thirteenth century, 52); and the cathedrals in Elgin and in Kirkwall (21), outside the area, also served parts of the Highlands. Other important centres of the medieval church were Iona (Argyll and Bute) with its abbey, Tain, Beauly and Portmahomack. On the west coast, the Celtic pattern of hermit-monks and travelling priests probably persisted. The absence of good building stone, and of suitable timber, in the west may have militated against durable building of churches, as of houses: buildings of unmortared beach or field-clearance boulders, with heather-thatched roofs, would have very limited lives. Throughout the western Highlands, there are slight

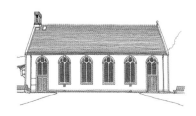

Fig. 15. Wardlaw Parish Church, Kirkhill,
Inverness-shire, Highland

remains of small chapels, and of the cells of hermit-monks, often in very remote locations.

The distinctive influence of the Irish-Celtic Church waned after a gathering of clergy – the Synod of Whitby – from various parts of what is now Britain agreed that the Roman form of Christianity should prevail; but it seems that, in remote parts of these islands, older forms continued. This is certainly the more recent experience, when major upheavals in church organisation and official belief have met with only partial acceptance in the Highlands (see below).

By the time the Reformation took place, in 1560, the eastern Highlands were firmly integrated into the Scottish kingdom; but in the west, and in some rural areas in the east, the 'Old Religion' persisted, often with the support of landowners. Though forced underground by penal laws, Roman Catholics in these areas have a continuity of worship in direct descent from the pre-Reformation Church, though there are no Roman Catholic places of worship surviving from that period. The monolithic Church of Scotland dominated the rest of the area until the rule of the Stuart dynasty as monarchs of the United Kingdom ended in 1689. The settlement reached in 1689, after William and Mary replaced James VII, established the Church of Scotland as a Presbyterian church in place of the Episcopal form of church government which had prevailed under James VI, Charles I, Charles II and James VII. In Aberdeenshire, Banffshire and Moray, many remained loyal to the Episcopal cause despite a degree of persecution which only subsided in the late eighteenth century.

Extreme Presbyterianism – Covenanting – did not take on in the Highlands. Nor, on the whole, did the Secessions from the Church of Scotland which took place during the eighteenth century in the Lowlands. These secessions were caused by concern about the legal right of landowners (and, in towns, town councils) to appoint parish ministers and otherwise to interfere with the Church. Continuing antagonism to this led in 1843 to a major split in the Church of Scotland – the Disruption – with the formation of the Free Church of Scotland. While the Church of Scotland's clergy and churches (and schoolmasters) were paid for by the landowners (and town councils), the Free Church

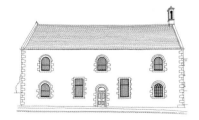

Fig. 16. The former North Free Church (ex-United Secession, now an evangelical church), Inverness, Highland

Fig. 17. The former Wick Old Parish Church
(now St Fergus), Caithness, Highland

had to raise the money to build churches and pay both ministers and schoolmasters. The Free Church was particularly warmly supported in the Highlands, where the influence of landowners had been resented for many years. The Disruption seriously weakened the Established Church of Scotland, which in the Highlands became a minority church. During the later nineteenth century, both the Roman Catholic and the Scottish Episcopal churches recolonised the Highlands.

In the late nineteenth century, there was a movement to amalgamate the Free Church with the United Presbyterian Church (itself a product of an earlier union of Secession churches). The United Presbyterians had never been strong in the Highlands. This union took place in 1900, forming the United Free Church of Scotland. Many Highland congregations of the Free Church stayed out of the union on doctrinal grounds. Similarly, when the United Free joined the Church of Scotland in 1929, some congregations, or parts of congregations, refused to join. An earlier split over doctrinal differences (in 1892) from the Free Church had resulted in the formation of the small Free Presbyterian Church of Scotland. This, in turn, split in 1989 over an issue of Church discipline, with the congregations who left forming a new body, the Associated Presbyterian Churches. Other denominations with churches in the Highlands include Baptists, Methodists, Congregationalists and various branches of the Christian Brethren, whose places of worship are known as gospel halls.

Before the Christianisation of Scotland, it is probable that sacredness was a property of places rather than buildings. The stone settings found in many parts of Scotland have recently been

Fig. 18. The former Loth Parish Church,
Lothmore, Sutherland, Highland

interpreted as having astronomical significance, but it is virtually certain that they had some sense of sacredness about them. The numerous burial cairns were probably also, to a degree, sacred places. To this day, places like the Ring of Brodgar, the Stones of Stenness (both in Orkney) and the amazing stone setting of Calanais (Callanish) on the Island of Lewis have a powerful sense of presence, as does the enigmatic 'Hill o' Many Stanes' in Caithness. The amount of effort needed to create the largest of these monuments strongly suggests a religious motive for their construction.

The earliest manifestations of Pictish religion in the Highlands are the simplest carved stones, with a fairly limited range of incised motifs. These include representations of bulls and horses, as well as more abstract symbols. Their function is not known, but they may well have been gathering points. The population which created them seems to have been a settled one, engaged in agriculture (hence the bulls and horses), and the cult they represent a fertility one. These abstract and animal motifs were succeeded by the second type of Pictish stone, which is characterised by the use of the cross as a motif, and by elaborate designs on the surfaces of the stones, incorporating interlace, zig-zag and spiral patterns, and sometimes raised bosses. Within the Highlands, these stones are particularly associated with Easter Ross, with collections in Rosemarkie (now in the Groam House Museum) and at Portmahomack (in Tarbat Old Parish Church). Other stones were in isolated settings, such as the Hilton of Cadboll stone (now in the National Museum of Scotland, Edinburgh) and the Shandwick and Nigg stones. The Hilton of Cadboll and Nigg stones are associated with later chapel sites, while the Shandwick Stone is on a hilltop, where it served as both a land and a sea mark. While the stone settings and cairns make their effect by scale and association with a remote, unknowable past, the later Pictish stones impress because of their artistic sophistication – an early example of a distinctive and complex Scottish achievement.

The church buildings of the Highlands are, apart from their religious significance, expressions of the economic and cultural contexts in which they have been, and are being, created – the building of churches in the Highlands continues. It is impossible to be comprehensive in a booklet of this length, so I have chosen themes which

Fig. 19. Duirinish Parish Church, Skye, Highland

Fig. 20. The former Ullapool Parish Church, Ross and Cromarty, Highland

seem to embody distinctively Highland characteristics. Many of the buildings mentioned are in Scotland's Churches Scheme (including a few no longer used regularly for worship), and details of them and of their opening arrangements are given in the gazetteer. Others are in regular use for worship, but may well be closed at other times.

Few in number and modest in scale, the medieval churches in the Highlands are nonetheless important reminders of a significant period in the history of the area. The medieval cathedrals of the Highlands – Fortrose, founded in the early twelfth century on the site of a Columban monastery, and Dornoch, founded in the thirteenth century (**52**) – survive in fragmentary form: Dornoch's choir was reused as the parish church after the Reformation in 1560, and the nave was not rebuilt until 1837. Fortrose's south aisle was kept as a burial aisle and restored as an Ancient Monument in 1852–3. The chapter-house at Fortrose with its vaulted undercroft is a precious survival. The twelfth-century ruined St Mary's Crosskirk, near Reay, Caithness, is probably typical of a number of small early medieval parish churches, its nave and choir layout contrasting with the single-chamber arrangement of many small west-coast churches. Part of Old St Peter's church in Thurso, also early, dating from the thirteenth century. There are remains of two monastic settlements in the area: Beauly Priory was founded in the thirteenth century, and its ruined church is still fairly complete. Fearn Abbey, a fourteenth-century foundation (**73**), fell into decay after the Reformation, but part of the abbey church was restored as a church in 1772, and is still in use as such. St Duthus, Tain, is a much-restored fifteenth-century building, now a museum, but originally a collegiate church staffed by a 'college' of priests. This was a type of religious house characteristic of the later pre-Reformation Church in Scotland. Some of the smaller post-Reformation buildings on the eastern seaboard

Fig. 21. Urquhart Parish Church, Drumnadrochit, Inverness-shire, Highland

also incorporate medieval fabric. Parts of the largely seventeenth-century Canisbay, Caithness (**42**), may date from the fifteenth century; and recent exploration of the fabric of Tarbat Old has suggested the reuse of older structures. Kincardine in Easter Ross is supposed, from its long, narrow plan, to be on medieval foundations.

The greatest medieval churches in northern Scotland, all well worth visiting, lie outside the Highlands. Iona Abbey, cradle of much of Highland Christianity, can be reached by tours from Oban, on the western seaboard, or by car and ferries from that town. Kirkwall's Norse cathedral, one of Scotland's greatest churches (**21**), on the Orkney Mainland, can be reached using a car ferry from Scrabster, near Thurso, Caithness, to Stromness. The third great medieval church is Elgin Cathedral, Moray, twenty-two miles east of Nairn. Its gaunt roofless remains, still richly carved, give a hint of the remarkable wealth of the province of Moray in the later medieval period. Finally, near the southern tip of Harris (which can be reached from mainland Scotland by car ferry from Uig, Skye, or Ullapool, Wester Ross) is a remarkable early sixteenth-century church, St Clement's, Rodel (**140**) totally unexpected in such a wild setting, and containing an extraordinarily richly carved mural tomb. These buildings provide an important context for the churches of the medieval Highlands mentioned above.

All along the eastern and north-eastern coastal strip of the Highlands, from Nairn to the north coast of Sutherland, is a series of post-Reformation churches of considerable distinction. Many are no longer places of worship, and some are roofless, but together they show that, from the early post-Reformation period, the area was prosperous and in full contact with the rest of 'Lowland' Scotland. They are all very simple, either long-rectangular or T-shaped in plan. Many have the plain rectangular windows which seem to have been normal for church buildings of the period from 1560 to about 1770, though some later buildings (or rebuildings) have round-headed windows and doorways. As a connected group, they are without parallel in Scotland and probably in Europe. They owe their relatively unaltered state to the hostility of most of the population to local landowners, which eventually found expression in the Disruption of 1843, when many left the Established Church of

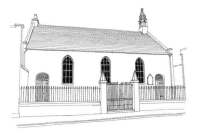

Fig. 22. Fort William Free Church, Inverness-shire, Highland

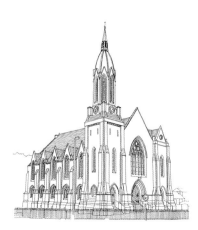

Fig. 23. Dingwall Free Church, Ross and Cromarty, Highland

Scotland for the Free Church. The result of this was that the older buildings remained adequate for the residual Established Church congregations.

There is still a feeling in the area against the 'Landowners' churches'. Fortunately, some have found new life after regular worship has ended, in the care of preservation trusts of one kind or another. Parts of Dunnet and of Cromarty East (**69**) date from the late sixteenth century, soon after the Reformation. Much of Nigg Old (1626, **81**), part of St Peter's Old, Thurso, and most of St Andrew's, Tongue (1680, **64**) and of the roofless Duirinish Old, Skye, survive to remind us of the seventeenth-century churches of the area. Two burial aisles, at Kilmuir Easter (1616, Fig. 10) and Kirkhill (1633, Fig. 11), survive as relics of the post-Reformation prohibition of burials inside churches, to illustrate seventeenth-century design and building techniques. Other important and distinctive parts of buildings survive from about 1700. These are the towers of Dunnet and Canisbay (1704, **42**) churches, and the unusually large belfry at Tarbat Old, Portmahomack, possibly designed as a lookout.

None of the churches so far mentioned (apart from Kirkwall and St Clement's, Rodel) survives in a form that enables its original appearance to be recreated with any degree of accuracy. The surviving evidence suggests, however, that the coastal strip, and some of the islands, were reasonably prosperous from the thirteenth to the seventeenth centuries, probably on account of their agricultural trade.

The political unrest which affected much of early eighteenth-

Fig. 24. Rosskeen Free Church, Ross and Cromarty, Highland

century Scotland, culminating in the Jacobite Rising of 1745-6, had relatively little impact on the eastern and northern Highlands, though elsewhere the building of roads and forts followed both that rising and the earlier one of 1715. There is an almost unbroken sequence of church-building, with little stylistic development, from the 1720s to the 1790s in the coastal area and in the area to the south-west of Inverness. Nigg Old was rebuilt into something like its present form in 1723-5 (**81**); and Contin also received major repairs in the eighteenth century (**68**). St Andrew's, Golspie (**55**) was built in stages between 1736 and the early 1750s, and has been little altered since. Edderton Old, built in 1743 (**54**), is similarly relatively unchanged. Tarbat Old and Cromarty East were both rebuilt in 1756, though the latter was again rebuilt in 1798-9 into its present form (**69**). Dunlichity (**94**) dates from 1759, though it incorporates sixteenth-century fabric. Croy and Dalcross (**89**) and Moy (**108**), though both somewhat altered, were originally constructed in the 1760s, as were the unique garrison church built in Fort George, Ardersier, in 1767 (**97**), and the parish church of Fort Augustus (1767, **96**), probably built partly as a garrison church.

The 1770s was an active period for church-building. Farr Old (1774), St Callan's, Rogart (1777, **61**), and Boleskine and Abertarff (1777, Fig. 12) all date from that decade, and Alness Old was rebuilt during that period. The 1780s was a difficult period, with harvest failures, but in 1783 both Urray (1775-83, Fig. 13) and Cromarty Gaelic Church (Fig. 14) were completed. In the early 1790s, Dalarossie (1790, **92**), Kirkhill (1790-2, Fig. 15) and Kingussie (1792, **112**) were constructed. In 1799, Kincardine was built or rebuilt on the long plan typical of the area, and in the same year the building of St Clement's, Dingwall (1799-1803, **70**), designed by an architect from East Lothian, in the Lowlands, was begun. The broad rectangular plan of the Dingwall church was a style used in the Lowlands since the 1750s, and its introduction marked the beginning of a process of integration of the Highlands into Lowland fashion – a process greatly assisted by improvements in transport and communications from the early nineteenth century.

In the later eighteenth century, economic necessity, and probably a desire for better living standards, encouraged migration from landward areas into towns and villages throughout Scotland. In

Fig. 25. Tain Parish Church (ex-Free), Ross and Cromarty, Highland

Fig. 26. Nairn Congregational Church
(now United Reformed Church), Highland

the Highlands, many of the people involved were Gaelic-speakers, and in a number of places churches were built for them. The older of the two surviving Highland examples is at Cromarty (1783, see Fig. 14), built for those who worked in a large hemp factory there. The other is in Inverness, where it was linked to the Old High Church (see below). Latterly used as Greyfriars Free Church, it is now a second-hand bookshop (1792–4, 1822).

As mentioned above, the eighteenth-century Secessions from the Church of Scotland had relatively little impact on the Highlands. In 1820, the larger part of the first Secession churches, which had fragmented during the eighteenth century, came together as the United Secession, which embarked on a programme of church-building. There are two examples in our area – in Inverness (1837, Fig. 16), which after a chequered history is now an evangelical church, and in Tain, now a Free Presbyterian church (see below).

During the first part of the nineteenth century, the Highlands had very mixed fortunes. In some areas, the migration from the landward areas continued, often with encouragement from landowners, and sometimes with a degree of coercion. This process involved both movement into towns and villages, and emigration, largely to the USA and Canada. Despite this migration, the Highland population continued to grow, and with it grew a need for new churches. With a very few exceptions, prior to the 1840s these new churches were provided in connection with the Church of Scotland. Some were in the expanding towns and villages, such as Wick Old (1820–30, Fig. 17) and Pulteneytown (1842, **47**), serving these two herring-fishing communities. Thurso St Peter's (1832, **45**) and Loth (1821–2, Fig. 18) were in the style of the First Gothic Revival, as were Rosemarkie (1818–21, **84**), St Andrew's Scottish

Fig. 27. Fortrose Free Church,
Ross and Cromarty, Highland

Episcopal church in Fortrose, and St Mary's Roman Catholic Church, Inverness (1837, **100**). The contemporary Roman Catholic Church of St Mun, Ballachulish (1836, **116**) is a simple structure to serve a congregation of slate quarrymen. Some churches in the west, including Clachan, Applecross (1817, **66**), Lochbroom Old and Lochcarron Old, show by their size the populated nature of areas that are now seriously depopulated. Other churches of this period, Daviot (1826, **93**) and Duirinish, Skye (1832, Fig. 19), are notably picturesque Georgian miniatures. The Church of Scotland in Broadford, Skye (1839–41, **130**) is much simpler. Cawdor, Nairnshire, was rebuilt in 1829–30 (**88**) in a consciously archaic style, incorporating parts of a church of 1619.

In the 1820s, the opening-up of the northern Highlands by the new roads constructed under the auspices of the Commissioners for Highland Roads and Bridges showed clearly that the growth in population in some parts of the Highlands and Islands had rendered church provision inadequate. Thomas Telford, consultant to the Commissioners, advised that some existing parishes should be split to form new 'Parliamentary parishes' with suitable church buildings and manses. This was approved by Parliament, and some sixteen Highland churches and manses were built to a more-or-less standard set of designs. Most of these churches still survive, but some have been rebuilt, and some have been converted for other uses. The church in Ullapool, Wester Ross, is a museum (1829, Fig. 20), and that at Strathy, Sutherland, a dwelling-house. A particularly poignant one is the church at Croick (1827, **51**), where comments by parishioners being cleared from Glen Calvie are scratched on the window panes. This church also retains its original fittings, including a transverse long communion table. Other surviving Telford churches include Berriedale, Sutherland; Duror (1827, **117**) and Ardgour (1829, **114**), Lochaber; Keiss, Caithness; and Plockton, Wester Ross. The 'Telford' churches at Strontian (1827–9, **128**) and Lochluichart (1825, **79**) have both been altered, the former radically. The vaguely 'Tudor' character of the 'Telford' churches is echoed in the more elaborate Urquhart, Drumnadrochit (1836–8, Fig. 21).

The impact of the Disruption of 1843 on the Church of Scotland has already been mentioned. In one instance, at Edderton, the Church of Scotland congregation had just moved to a new building, and the Free Church took over

Fig. 28. Inverallan Parish Church, Grantown-on-Spey, Inverness-shire, Highland

Fig. 29. The former Golspie United Free Church, Sutherland, Highland

the old parish church (1743, **54**). Elsewhere, simple new buildings were constructed, at least at first. Early examples survive at Bernisdale, Skye (1843–7); Fort William, Lochaber (1846, Fig. 22); and Portree (now Church of Scotland, 1854, **134**). Small Free churches continued to be built to serve country areas, such as at Altnaharra, Sutherland; Resolis, Easter Ross (1865); and Croy and Dalcross, Nairnshire. Some were built as mission churches, such as Strathnaver (1901, **63**) and Arnisort, Skye.

The great stronghold of the Free Church in the Highlands was Inverness, whose churches will be discussed below. As the nineteenth century wore on, prosperity in the eastern Highlands resulted in the replacement of earlier Free churches by larger and more elaborate ones, usually in the then-fashionable Gothic Revival style. Examples of the largest Gothic Free churches outside Inverness are in Invergordon (1859–61); Dingwall (1867–70, Fig. 23); Rosskeen (c. 1870, Fig. 24); Nairn (1880–2); Strathpeffer (1886); and Fortrose (1895–8, **74**). Smaller Gothic Revival Free churches include Killearnan (1864) and Gairloch (1878, **75**) both Ross and Cromarty. Another favoured style was Italianate, as seen in the remote Caithness church of Halkirk (1884–6, **43**). Larger buildings in a similar style are in Tain (1891–2, Fig. 25) and the former Queen Street Free Church in Inverness (1893–6). Minority Protestant denominations were represented in the larger towns. An example of a Congregational church is in Nairn (1860–1, Fig. 26).

The union of much of the Free Church with the United Presbyterian Church in 1900 placed some of the former Free churches in the hands of the new United Free Church; and most of these came to the Church of Scotland when

Fig. 30. Stratherrick Free Presbyterian Church, Inverness-shire, Highland

that Church united with the United Free in 1929. Hence, for example, the churches at Fortrose, Nairn, Invergordon, Tain and Halkirk are now Church of Scotland buildings. Free North, Inverness (1890–3, **103**), Killearnan and Rosskeen are instances of large Free churches remaining in the ownership of that denomination. There are also examples of Free churches built after 1900 for breakaway parts of congregations, for instance at Fortrose (early twentieth century, Fig. 27), and a larger one in Nairn (1908–9). New Free churches are still being built, mostly modest in scale and simple in design, as at North Kessock in the Black Isle, and in Caol near Fort William.

Most of the large churches constructed in the Highlands between 1843 and 1900 were Free churches. One exception was St Andrew's Scottish Episcopal Cathedral, Inverness (1866–9, **99**). Another was the church of Fort Augustus Abbey (begun 1890, not completed until 1980). Only a handful of large churches were built during this period by the Church of Scotland. These were Avoch (1870–2, **67**); Duncansburgh, Fort William (1881); Strathpeffer, now Fodderty and Strathpeffer (1888–90, **85**); Nairn Old (1895–7, **90**); and St Stephen's, Inverness (1897, **106**), a daughter church of the Old High. These are all of distinctive and original designs, with no obvious parallels elsewhere in the Highlands, though Nairn Old is very similar to a church in Kelso.

Smaller Church of Scotland buildings continued to be constructed after the Disruption. Early examples include Glencoe St Munda's (1845, **115**), built for Ballachulish quarrymen; Bower, Caithness (1847, **41**); and Lairg, Sutherland (1847, **57**). Later examples are Altnaharra, Sutherland (1854–7, **49**); Glengarry (1864–7, **120**), enlarged in 1896–7; the very simple Kyleakin, Skye (1875, **133**); and the mildly Gothic Kilmore, Skye (1876–7, **132**). Inverallan, Grantown-on-Spey (1884–6, Fig. 28) was built as a memorial to the seventh and eighth earls of Seafield and is a most unusual building. Three of the windows have tracery incorporating the initials of the earls and of the seventh earl's widow – a 'landowner's' church indeed.

In 1899–1901, St Andrew's, Aviemore (**110**) was built to serve a community expanded by the building of the direct railway to Inverness. At about the same time, a small Arts and Crafts church was built at Lochaline, Morvern (1898, **124**), and mission churches were constructed at Kingairloch (**121**) and Tomdoun (**129**), also in Lochaber.

Fig. 31. St John's Roman Catholic Church, Caol, Inverness-shire, Highland

Fig. 32. St Columba's Scottish Episcopal Church, Brora, Sutherland, Highland

The newly formed United Free Church saw after 1900 a need for church buildings to serve areas where population had expanded in the late nineteenth century, and also in places where the Free churches had stayed out of the Union. Most of the new buildings in the Highlands were similar in style and size – small Perpendicular Gothic churches, without spires, often with manses within the same building plot. Examples include Portmahomack (1908, **83**); Farr, Bettyhill (1909, **50**); Strathy (1910, **62**); Thrumster (1910, **44**); Pitfure, Rogart (1910, **60**); and Lochcarron West (1910, **78**). Larger United Free churches built as such can be seen at Crown (1900–1, **102**) and Ness Bank (1900–1, **105**) churches, Inverness (both planned before the Union); at Golspie (1905–6, Fig. 29); and at Castle Street, Dingwall (1909). The Golspie church is now a hall. Most of the church buildings constructed by the United Free Church came into the Church of Scotland in 1929, together with those Free churches which had entered the Union of 1900.

As mentioned above, the Free Presbyterian Church broke away from the Free Church in 1892 over doctrinal differences. It has remained a small denomination, and most of its churches are small. Some were taken over from other denominations, such as the former United Secession church in Tain. Two examples of churches built specifically for the Free Presbyterians are in Inverness (1899) and Stratherrick (1899, Fig. 30). In 1989, the Free Presbyterians themselves split, the congregations which left (including the Inverness one) joining together as the Associated Presbyterian Churches.

The Roman Catholic Church was outlawed in Scotland for most of the period from the Reformation until the late eighteenth century, latterly because of the perceived risk of a third Jacobite rising. The first two Jacobite risings, in 1715 and 1745–6, had been linked with Roman Catholicism and France. Catholicism had not, however, died out. In remote parts of the western Highlands and Islands, and in upland Aberdeenshire and Banff-shire, the 'Old Religion' was kept up. There was a Catholic church at Dornie in 1703; and soon after that, in 1716, a secret seminary was established at Scalan, in upland Banffshire, to train boys for the priesthood. A new building was constructed at Scalan in 1762–7, and this still survives and can be visited.

The oldest surviving Catholic church in the Highlands is the Italianate St Mary's, Eskadale, Inverness-shire (1825–6, **95**), built by a local landowner. This was followed in the 1830s by the Gothic St Mary's, Inverness (1836–7, **100**) and the classical St Joachim's, Wick (1836–7), both designed by the same architect, William Robertson. Later in the nineteenth century, several new churches were built for the Catholic congregations in the Highlands. Some, as at St Duthac's, Dornie (1860, **72**) and Our Lady and St Cumin, Morar (1889, **126**), replaced earlier buildings; and others, including St Mary's, Beauly (1864, **91**), Our Lady and St Bean, Marydale (1868, **80**) and St Mary and St Finnan, Glenfinnan (1872, **119**), were new foundations. More were constructed in the twentieth century, including the fine St Mary's, Fort William (1933–4, **118**); St Patrick's, Mallaig (1935, **125**); St John the Evangelist, Caol (a suburb of Fort William) (1970, Fig. 31); and in Thurso, Caithness, to serve people brought to these places by industrial growth. Industrial growth also led the Church of Scotland to build Kinlochleven (1930, **122**) to serve workers at the aluminium smelter in that isolated village.

The Scottish Episcopal Church in its present form, as mentioned earlier, was initially a remnant of the pre-1690 Church of Scotland. Like the Roman Catholic Church, it was outlawed until the late eighteenth century. An early nineteenth-century example of a Scottish Episcopal church is in Fortrose (1828). After that, the influence of the Church of England on its liturgy and church buildings became increasingly strong, though unlike the latter it remained independent of state influence. The Oxford Movement, with its emphasis on a return to medieval forms of worship and church design, influenced the Episcopal Church in Scotland in the mid-nineteenth century. An early example of such a church in the Highlands is St James the Great, Dingwall (1854, **71**). In 1869, St Andrew's Cathedral in Inverness (**99**) was completed (apart from its spires), and the diocese of which it was the centre established many new churches throughout the Highlands. Most of these were fairly small, with a nave and chancel, but were relatively richly furnished, in comparison with the plainness of contemporary Church of Scotland and Free churches. Good examples mentioned in the gazetteer are the churches of St Finan, Kinlochmoidart (1857–60, **123**); St John the Evangelist, Wick (1870, **48**); St

Fig. 33. Barra Parish Church, Cuier, Barra, Western Isles

Fig. 34. Lochmaddy Parish Church, North Uist, Western Isles

Columba, Portree (1884, **135**); St Andrew, Tain (1887, **87**); and St Finnbarr, Dornoch (1912–13, **53**). More elaborate ones, with small spires, are St Peter and the Holy Rood, Thurso (1883–4, **46**), and St Anne, Strathpeffer (1890–9, **86**). An Arts and Crafts example of the smaller type is St Columba, Grantown-on-Spey (1892–3, **111**).

Few Episcopal churches have been built since the First World War. Of these, the most interesting architecturally is St John the Baptist, Rothiemurchus (1928–9, **113**). The most unusual is the tiny St Donnan, Lochalsh (1962–4, **77**), built by a single family during successive summer holidays. The little St Maelrubha, Poolewe (1965, **82**) was converted from a cow byre. The Lochalsh and Poolewe churches are the first Episcopal churches built in the area since 1690.

Inverness is notable for the way in which the River Ness flows through the heart of the city. The freshness and lightness which this affords is complemented by a unique concentration of church buildings flanking the river. Some are no longer in Church use, but all add distinctively to the character of the city. Their number (and the size of many of them) clearly indicates the importance of the place, especially since the mid-nineteenth century. The most striking members of the group are three on the east bank – the Old High (tower sixteenth century, body 1769–72, **98**), Free North (1890–3, **103**) and St Columba's High (formerly Free High) (1851–2, rebuilt after a fire, 1948–53). Of these, the Old High, the oldest church in the city, is distinctive in having a tower, with a bellcote on top. Free North (sometimes described as 'the Free Church Cathedral') has a spire of great height and extraordinary complexity. St Columba's spire lost its flying buttresses in a fire in 1939, but is still most impressive. Facing this trio is a very different group of churches: the 'College Chapel' Gothic St Mary's Catholic (1836–7, **100**) at the south end; then the simple classicism of the former West Church of Scotland, now residential (1837–40); and finally the striking Italianate of the former Queen Street Free Church (1893–6), now a funeral parlour.

This wonderful core group of six churches is complemented by others up- and downstream, and behind the waterfronts. Upstream are the little Tweedmouth Memorial Chapel (1896–8, **107**) of the Royal Northern Infirmary (west bank) and, as mentioned above, the richly detailed late Gothic Revival Ness Bank Church of Scotland (east bank) (1900–1, **105**) and the twin-towered

Fig. 35. Martin's Memorial Church of Scotland (ex-English Free), Stornoway, Western Isles

St Andrew's Scottish Episcopal Cathedral (west bank) (1866-9, **99**), embowered in trees. Downstream are the former Free plain-gabled Trinity Church of Scotland (1863) and the quietly modern Inverness Methodist Church (1964-5, **104**), built to replace one destroyed by fire. To the east of the Old High is the former Greyfriars Free (1792-4, 1822), built as a church for Gaelic-speakers, and now a second-hand bookshop; and on College Street, farther east, is the simple Georgian-revival Free Presbyterian church (1899). Tucked in behind this is the first Free North Church, built as a United Secession church (see above; 1837, Fig. 21), and taken over as a Free church after 1843. It is now an evangelical church.

On the west bank, behind the former West Church of Scotland, is the Scottish Episcopal Church of St Michael and All Angels (1903-4, **101**), the epitome of a small Episcopal church. In the hinterland to the east of Ness Bank are three more: the simple, harled Baptist church; the Gothic Revival Crown Church of Scotland, built as a United Free Church after the union of 1900 (1900-1, **102**); and St Stephen's, a daughter church of the Old High, an Arts and Crafts Gothic building, unusual for the Highlands (1897, **106**).

Behind this most eclectic set of frontages, which give Inverness a unique character, are interiors (in many cases) which epitomise the approaches to worship of the different Churches: in the Catholic and Episcopal Churches the 'House of God', home of the blessed Sacrament, and in the Presbyterian and Methodist churches places for the preaching of the Word. There are no organs in the Free or the Free Presbyterian churches. Because so many of the churches are members of Scotland's Churches Scheme, there is an unusual opportunity for visitors to see something of the wonderful variety of 'sacred spaces' in the 'Capital of the Highlands' and to appreciate the distinctive characters of the Churches which have been responsible for their creation.

An interesting and distinctive type of church found in many parts of the Highlands is the prefabricated building, made in parts in factories,

Fig. 36. Stornoway Free Church, Western Isles

usually in Glasgow, and shipped up. They were often put up in sparsely populated places, or as temporary accommodation, with the intention that they would be replaced by masonry structures in a few years. Though their numbers are diminishing, there are a fair number still in use for worship, by several denominations. Tomatin, Inverness-shire (1910, **109**) and Elgol, Skye (1898, **131**) are in Scotland's Churches Scheme, and other examples are the former Stratherrick Church of Scotland (early twentieth century), the Evangelical Free church at Canisbay (early twentieth century) and St Columba's Episcopal Church, Brora (1909, Fig. 32).

The Western Isles

Sometimes referred to as the 'Long Island', this archipelago includes the largest island off the coast of Britain – Lewis and Harris – as well as a large number of smaller islands, most of them now uninhabited. As in Orkney, prehistoric people seem to have had a strong religious sense, most clearly expressed in the stone setting at Callanish, on the west coast of Lewis, and in a large number of chambered tombs. The islands appear to have been Christianised by Irish-Celtic missionaries – and one of the oldest places of worship still in use, at Eoropaidh, Lewis (thirteenth century, **136**), is a little Scottish Episcopal church dedicated to St Moluag. Its design seems to have parallels with a Norse cathedral in Greenland. Another early church is the North Chapel, Cille Bharra, Eoligarry, Barra (twelfth century, **152**). Notable among the ruined chapels is the Teampull na Trionaidh (Church of the Holy Trinity) at Carinish, North Uist, supposed to date from the twelfth century. There is also an interesting group of ruined chapels at Howmore, South Uist. As mentioned above, the only large pre-Reformation church in the area is St Clement's, Rodel, Harris (early sixteenth century, **140**), a building of great dignity, and so sited as to be a pilgrimage church.

After the Reformation, the north isles (North Uist, Berneray, Harris and Lewis, plus some smaller islands) embraced the Reformed religion, but the south isles (Benbecula, South Uist, Eriskay, Barra, Vatersay and some smaller islands) retained the 'Old Religion' (Roman Catholicism). The standard of living in the islands was by mainland standards poor, with much subsistence farming; and many of the inhabitants emigrated to the mainland or to North America from the early nineteenth century, some forcibly cleared from the land. The improvement of agriculture (including the confirmation of crofting tenure from 1886), some modest industry, and lobster and herring-fishing brought a measure of prosperity to all the islands in the later nineteenth century, and the organisation of the traditional wool-weaving industry to produce 'Harris Tweed' retained population in the crofting townships.

The Disruption was warmly welcomed in the Protestant north isles, and the Free Church became a powerful influence on the area. The role of the urban Free Church in relieving the potato famine in the western Highlands probably helped to earn the loyalty of the islanders, and the influence of a succession of landowners who came from outside the area no doubt stiffened antagonism to the Established Church of Scotland – the 'landowners' church'. When the bulk of the Free Church amalgamated with the United Presbyterian Church in 1900 to form the United Free Church, many of the island Free churches remained outside the Union, and to this day Lewis and Harris remain strongholds of the Free Church. When in 1892 the Free Presbyterian Church split from the Free Church, again the islanders were among the strongest supporters of the new Church. The split in the Free Presbyterians in 1989 also affected the islands. The separateness of these denominations from others in the islands is a distinctive feature of the Western Isles, reflected in their strong Sabbatarian beliefs and in their strict beliefs about state involvement in religion. There are no island churches of these denominations in Scotland's Churches Scheme.

Apart from the restored early medieval buildings referred to earlier, the churches in use in the Western Isles are with one exception later than 1800. That exception is St Columba's (Old Parish) Church, Stornoway (**137**), which was originally built in 1794 when the town was being laid out

Fig. 37. Free Presbyterian Church, Stornoway, Western Isles

as a model settlement. In its present condition, it reflects the alterations made in 1831 and 1884–5, the last when the town was a major centre for herring-fishing. When the township on St Kilda was remodelled in the early nineteenth century, a small, plain church (**155**) was built. Abandoned when the island was evacuated in 1930, it has in recent years been restored as an inter-denominational worship space. The parish church on Barra was built in 1829–34 (Fig. 33) and is a simple building, as are the Church of Scotland churches of Howmore, South Uist (1858, **148**) and Carinish, North Uist (1867, **143**). Howmore and Carinish both have long communion tables, rare survivals from the once-common practice of communicants moving to sit at a table to receive the bread and wine during the celebration of the Sacrament.

The Free Church was very active in church-building, as already implied; and, though many Free Church congregations did not come into the Union of 1900, some did, their church buildings then transferring to the Church of Scotland in 1929. Examples include the churches at Daliburgh, South Uist (1862–3, **145**), on Berneray (1887, **141**), and at Clachan (1889, **144**) and Lochmaddy, North Uist (1891, Fig. 34). These are all simple buildings, but Martin's Memorial Church in Stornoway, originally the town's English Free Church (1876–8, Fig. 35), is in Gothic Revival style. Its steeple, planned from the beginning, was added in 1910. Kilmuir Church, North Uist (1892–4, **142**) is in a simpler Gothic. The Free Church in Kenneth Street, Stornoway (1851, Fig. 36), in a simple early Gothic style, is included here to represent that denomination. So, too, is the early twentieth-century Free Presbyterian Church in Matheson Road, Stornoway (Fig. 37), in a distinctive version of Romanesque.

As described above, the south isles are largely Roman Catholic. The oldest church of that denomination still in use is St Brendan, Barra (1805, **150**), a simple building. St Mary's, Bornish, South Uist (1837, Fig. 38) was originally like that, but was adapted in 1955, with an apsidal baptistery. Our Lady Star of the Sea, Castlebay, Barra, is the largest Roman Catholic church in the islands, with a tower (1886, **149**). The little church of St Michael, on the small island of Eriskay (1903, Fig. 39), is a delight, entirely appropriate to its remote setting. It was followed in 1906 by St Barr's, Northbay, Barra (**153**). Since the Second World War, the Roman Catholic Church has built four new churches in the Western Isles. St Vincent de Paul, Eoligarry, Barra (1964, **151**) is a modern version of the simple gabled church, but in

Fig. 38. St Mary's Roman Catholic Church, Bornish, South Uist, Western Isles

Fig. 39. St Michael's Roman Catholic Church, Eriskay, Western Isles

the following year the remarkable Our Lady of Sorrows was built at Garrynamonie, South Uist (147), a fine example of a modernist church of the period – I suggest architecturally one of the best small Scottish churches of the second half of the twentieth century. The more recent Our Lady of the Waves and St John, Vatersay (154) and Church of Our Holy Redeemer, Stornoway (138) are simple, workmanlike buildings. The ramped access to the latter, very much of its period, is an important element in its design.

In conclusion, one can with justification say that the church history of the Highlands and Islands is a distinctive and important one, to be seen against a background of pre-Christian notions of the sacred. Visiting Highland and island churches, in use for worship or not, gives a very powerful sense of continuity with a past inhabited by the many generations who moved into and out of the area over many centuries. The churches and their graveyards evoke a whole succession of vanished pasts: the missionary journeys of remembered and unremembered saints; the building skills of long-gone craftsmen; the faithful ministry of priests, ministers and ordinary worshippers; echoes of old – and not-so-old – theological disputes; love of God and love of neighbour. All of these can be seen as aspects of the sacred.

Perception of sacredness in past or present places of worship is not to be equated with heritage or nostalgia. It is indeed a way of linking with the generations of faithful people who have worshipped in them. Of much more fundamental importance, it is an awakening or confirmation of a non-material but transcendentally important dimension of our lives – the spiritual.

PROFESSOR JOHN R. HUME
Universities of Glasgow and St Andrews

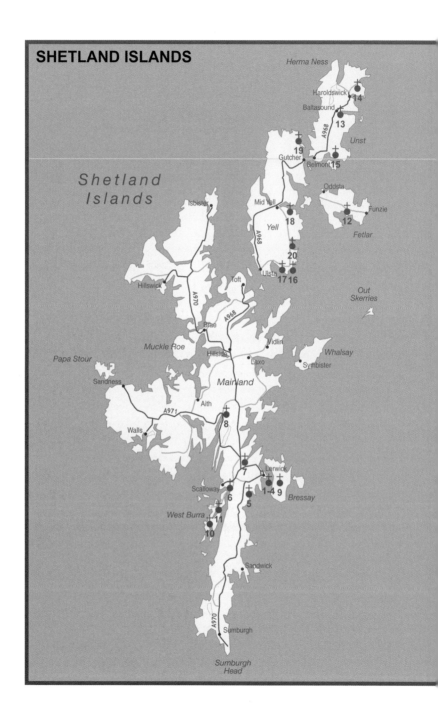

SHETLAND ISLANDS

Herma Ness

Haroldswick
Baltasound
13 **14**
A968
19 Unst
Gutcher **15**
Belmont

Oddsta
Mid Yell
18 Funzie
Yell **12**
A968 Fetlar

20
Ulsta **17 16**
Out
Skerries

Isbister

*Shetland
Islands*

Hillswick Toft
A970
Brae
A968
Vidlin
Muckle Roe
Hillside Whalsay
Laxo Symbister

Papa Stour
Sandness *Mainland*
A971
Aith
Walls **8**

Lerwick
7
Scalloway **1-4 9**
6 *Bressay*
West Burra **5**
11
10

Sandwick

A970
Sumburgh

*Sumburgh
Head*

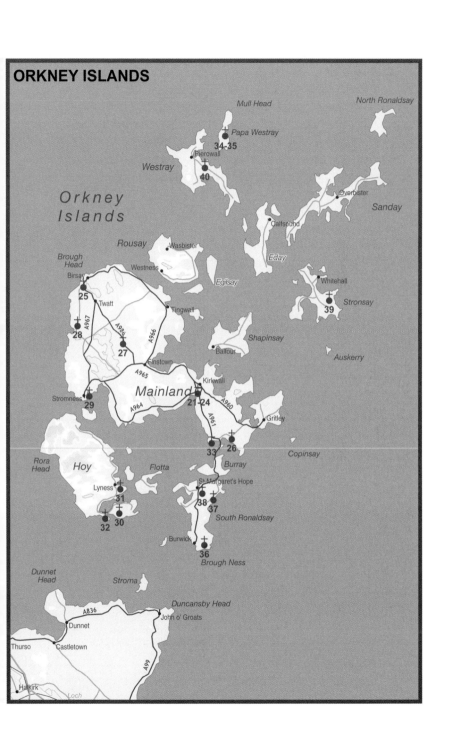

ORKNEY ISLANDS

Mull Head

North Ronaldsay

Papa Westray

34-35

Pierowall

40

Westray

Orkney
Islands

Overbister

Sanday

Calfsound

Rousay

Wasbister

Eday

Brough
Head

Westness

Birsay

Egilsay

Whitehall

Stronsay

25

Twatt

39

A967

A986

Tingwall

A966

28

Shapinsay

27

Balfour

Auskerry

Finstown

A965

Kirkwall

Mainland

Stromness

A964

21-24

A960

29

A961

Gritley

Copinsay

33

26

Rora
Head

Hoy

Flotta

Burray

St Margaret's Hope

Lyness

31

38 **37**

32 **30**

South Ronaldsay

Burwick

36

Brough Ness

Dunnet
Head

Stroma

Duncansby Head

A836

John o' Groats

Dunnet

Thurso

Castletown

A99

Halkirk

Loch

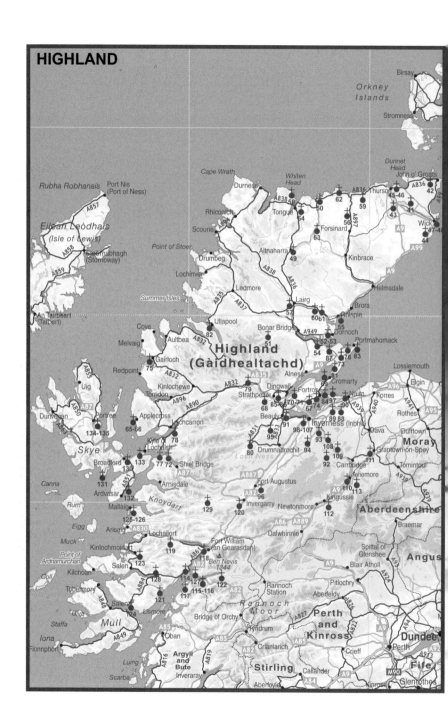

HIGHLAND

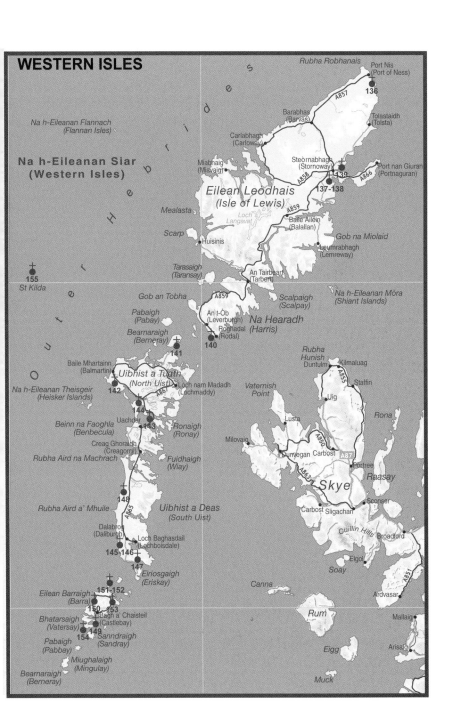

WESTERN ISLES

Na h-Eileanan Flannach
(Flannan Isles)

Na h-Eileanan Siar
(Western Isles)

Rubha Robhanais

Port Nis
(Port of Ness)

136

A857

Barabhas
(Barvas)

Tolastaidh
(Tolsta)

Carlabhagh
(Carloway)

Miabhaig
(Miavaig)

Steòrnabhagh
(Stornoway)

Port nan Giuran
(Portnaguran)

A858

139

A866

137-138

Eilean Leòdhais
(Isle of Lewis)

Mealasta

A859

Loch
Langavat

Baile Ailein
(Balallan)

Scarp

Huisinis

Gob na Miolaid

Leumrabhagh
(Lemreway)

Tarasaigh
(Taransay)

An Tairbeart
(Tarbert)

155
St Kilda

Gob an Tobha

A859

Scalpaigh
(Scalpay)

Na h-Eileanan Mòra
(Shiant Islands)

Pabaigh
(Pabay)

An t-Òb
(Leverburgh)

Na Hearadh
(Harris)

Bearnaraigh
(Berneray)

Roghadal
(Rodal)

141

140

Rubha
Hunish

Duntulm

Kilmaluag

Baile Mhartainn
(Balmartin)

Uibhist a Tuath
(North Uist)

Loch nam Madadh
(Lochmaddy)

A855

Staffin

142

A861

Vaternish
Point

Uig

Na h-Eileanan Theisgeir
(Heisker Islands)

144

Rona

Beinn na Faoghla
(Benbecula)

Uachdar

143

Ronaigh
(Ronay)

Lusta

Creag Ghoraidh
(Creagorry)

Rubha Aird na Machrach

Fuidhaigh
(Wiay)

Milovaig

A850

Carbost

Dunvegan

A87

Portree

Raasay

A863

Skye

148

A865

Uibhist a Deas
(South Uist)

Carbost

Sligachan

Sconser

Rubha Aird a' Mhuile

Cuillin Hills

Broadford

Dalabrog
(Daliburgh)

Loch Baghasdail
(Lochboisdale)

145-146

Elgol

147

Eiriosgaigh
(Eriskay)

Soay

A851

Canna

Eilean Barraigh
(Barra)

151-152

150

153

Ardvasar

Rum

Mallaig

Bhatarsaigh
(Vatersay)

Bagh a' Chaisteil
(Castlebay)

149

154

Sanndraigh
(Sandray)

Pabaigh
(Pabbay)

Arisaig

Miughalaigh
(Mingulay)

Eigg

Bearnaraigh
(Berneray)

Muck

How to use this Guide

Entries are arranged by local-authority area, with large areas sub-divided for convenience. The number preceding each entry refers to the map. Each entry is followed by symbols for access and facilities:

Å	Ordnance Survey reference	∂	Hearing induction loop for the deaf
♨	Denomination	☺	Welcomers and guides on duty
⊕	Church website	📖	Guidebooks and souvenirs available/for sale
●	Regular services		
○	Church events	NADFAS	Church Recorders' Inventory (NADFAS)
●	Opening arrangements		
♿	Wheelchair access for partially abled	▆	Refreshments
WC	Toilets available for visitors	A	Category A listing
		B	Category B listing
WC	Toilets adapted for the disabled available for visitors	C	Category C listing

Category A: Buildings of national or international importance, either architectural or historic, or fine little-altered examples of some particular period, style or building type.

Category B: Buildings of regional or more than local importance, or major examples of some particular period, style or building type which may have been altered.

Category C: Buildings of local importance, lesser examples of any period, style, or building type, as originally constructed or moderately altered; and simple traditional buildings which group well with others in categories A and B.

The information appearing in the gazetteer of this guide is supplied by the participating churches. While this is believed to be correct at the time of going to press, Scotland's Churches Scheme cannot accept any responsibility for its accuracy.

SHETLAND

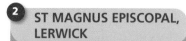

❶ ST COLUMBA'S, LERWICK

**1 Greenfield Place
Lerwick
ZE1 0AQ**

🏔 HU 478 411

⛪ Church of Scotland

🌐 www.shetlandcommunities.org/
lbpc/

Linked with Gulberwick (5), Bressay (9)

Designed by James Milne of Edinburgh and built 1828 with interior and apse of 1895 by John M. Aitken, the church is recognised as a fine example of neo-classical architecture in the north of Scotland. Splendid horseshoe gallery. Organ by Bryceson Bros of London, 1871. Stained-glass window depicting the figure of Jesus by Danish sculptor Thorvaldsen. Extensive refurbishment in 2008.

- Sunday: 11.15am
- Open by arrangement (01595 692125)

❷ ST MAGNUS EPISCOPAL, LERWICK

**Greenfield Place
Lerwick
ZE1 0AQ**

🏔 HU 479 411

⛪ Scottish Episcopal

🌐 www.stmagnus.org.uk

Linked with St Colman's, Yell (16)

Designed by Alexander Ellis in Early English style and built 1862–4. Battlemented tower added 1891. Alterations to chancel by Alexander Ross, 1899. Windows by Sir Ninian Comper (moved here from the chapel of the former House of Charity in 1973).

- Sunday: 10.45am and 6.30pm; Monday to Friday: as advertised
- Open daily (01595 693862)

3 ST MARGARET'S CHURCH, LERWICK

**Harbour Street
Lerwick
ZE1 0ES**

⚐ HU 473 415

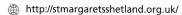 Roman Catholic

⊕ http://stmargaretsshetland.org.uk/

Corner of St Olaf Street

When St Margaret's was opened in 1911, it was described as 'the prettiest church in Lerwick'. The architect was James Baikie of Kirkwall. One of the outstanding features is the high altar, carved out of Belgian oak. The church is dominated by three large stained-glass windows by C. R. Sinclair, 1986, depicting traditional and contemporary life in Shetland.

- Saturday: 5.00pm; Sunday: 10.30am
- Open daily 8.00am–8.00pm (01595 692233)

4 ADAM CLARKE MEMORIAL METHODIST CHURCH, LERWICK

**Hillhead
Lerwick
ZE1 0EJ**

⚐ HU 475 412

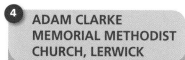 Methodist

Linked with Haroldswick Methodist, Unst (14), East Yell Methodist (20)

Built 1872 and named after Rev. Adam Clarke (1760–1832), President of the Wesleyan Methodist Conference, who greatly encouraged the development of Methodism in Shetland. Major refurbishment in 1994. Stained-glass window in memory of William Goudie, a Shetlander designated President of the Wesleyan Methodist Conference in 1922, who died before taking office.

- Sunday: 11.00am and 6.15pm
- Open by arrangement (01595 692874)

SHETLAND

⑤ GULBERWICK CHURCH

Gulberwick
ZE2 9JX

🏹 HU 443 389

⛪ Church of Scotland

🌐 www.shetlandcommunities.org/lbpc/

Linked with St Columba's, Lerwick (1), Bressay (9)

3km (2 miles) south of Lerwick

A handsome and simple church built in 1898 with Orkney stone facings. The windows behind the pulpit are filled with cathedral squares. Picturesquely situated in the village of Gulberwick with a graveyard overlooking the sea.

- Sunday: 10.00am
- Open by arrangement (01595 692125)

⑥ SCALLOWAY CHURCH

Main Street
Scalloway
ZE1 0TR

🏹 HU 401 395

⛪ Church of Scotland

🌐 www.burratingwall.org.uk/

Linked with Tingwall (7), Weisdale (8), Bridge End, Burra (10), Meal Kirk, Burra (11)

Close to West Shore

Scalloway Kirk, built in 1840–1, is a two-storey square building with a piended roof and a bellcote above the entrance porch. The white-painted horseshoe gallery and pews and red carpets make the interior bright and welcoming. The organ is one of only four pipe organs remaining in Shetland, thought to be by Andrew Watt of Glasgow in 1902.

- Sunday: 10.45am, except 5th Sunday of the month, when a charge-wide united service is held (see local press or website)
- Open by arrangement (01595 881157)

7 TINGWALL CHURCH

St Magnus

**Tingwall
ZE2 9SB**

⚐ HU 419 438

⌂ Church of Scotland

🌐 www.burratingwall.org.uk/

Linked with Scalloway (6), Weisdale (8), Bridge End, Burra (10), Meal Kirk, Burra (11)

On B9074 at north end of Loch of Tingwall

Typical white-harled hall-church of the Reformed tradition, this is the second-oldest church in Shetland still in use. It opened in 1790, although there has been a church in Tingwall since the 12th century. Part of the old church may still be seen in the nearby grass-covered burial vault. Inside, the church still has its original late 18th-century interior with gallery and tall pulpit.

- Sunday: 9.15am April to September, 12.00 noon October to March, except 5th Sunday of the month, when a charge-wide united service is held (see local press or website)
- Open daily (01595 881157)

8 WEISDALE CHURCH

**Weisdale
ZE2 9LW**

⚐ HU 394 526

⌂ Church of Scotland

🌐 www.burratingwall.org.uk/

Linked with Scalloway (6), Tingwall (7), Bridge End, Burra (10), Meal Kirk, Burra (11)

On B9075, close to junction with A971

Built as a Free Church in 1863, allocated to the United Free Church in 1908, finally Church of Scotland in 1929. Symmetrical hall-church with Gothic details and a birdcage bellcote. The original interior survives, including a combined pulpit and lectern with fine wood carving. With the support of the *Beechgrove Garden* television programme, a community garden was created in 2005.

- Sunday: 10.30am, except 5th Sunday of the month, when a charge-wide united service is held (see local press or website)
- Open daily (01595 881157)

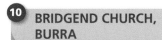

9 BRESSAY CHURCH

Bressay
ZE2 9EL

⚇ HU 493 410
🏠 Church of Scotland
🌐 www.shetlandcommunities.org/lbpc/

Linked with St Columba's, Lerwick (1), Gulberwick (5)

1.6km (1 mile) south from ferry

A typical harled kirk with belfry of the early 19th century, built 1812 to replace an earlier kirk of 1722 which in turn replaced Bressay's three ancient chapels. The church boasts two beautiful stained-glass windows, 1895, of St Peter and St Paul. At each of the windows are memorial tablets. The church overlooks the bay and its seals.

- Sunday: 3.00pm
- Open by arrangement (01595 692125)

10 BRIDGEND CHURCH, BURRA

Bridge End
ZE2 9LD

⚇ HU 375 331
🏠 Church of Scotland
🌐 www.burratingwall.org.uk/

Linked with Scalloway (6), Tingwall (7), Weisdale (8), Meal Kirk, Burra (11)

At bridge between East and West Burra

Built 1865 as a United Presbyterian Church, amalgamated with the United Free Church in 1900 and became part of the Church of Scotland in 1929. Church and attached manse were built together, the church looking almost like a cottage apart from the bellcote on the gable.

- Sunday: 12.30pm every fortnight (check website)
- Open by arrangement (01595 859517)

11 MEAL KIRK, BURRA

Meal

Hamnavoe
ZE2 9LB

HU 376 357

Church of Scotland

www.burratingwall.org.uk/

Linked with Scalloway (6), Tingwall
(7), Weisdale (8), Bridge End, Burra
(10)

B9074

Built 1907 as a mission church of the
Church of Scotland. Small grey-harled
church with white-painted window
surrounds and quoins. Simple
bellcote on east gable. Improvements
are planned to increase use of the
building by the community.

- Sunday: 6.00pm every fortnight
  (check website)
- Open by arrangement (01595 859517)

12 FETLAR PARISH CHURCH

Tresta
Fetlar
ZE2 9DJ

HU 608 905

Church of Scotland

Follow signs for Tresta

The present building was erected
in 1790 and recast 1860; there are
medieval masonry remains under the
foundations. Traditional hall-church
of rectangular plan and harled walls.
Coloured glass windows, restored
2009. Walled burial grounds include
Cheyne and Nicholson families. The
oldest memorial is set in the wall of
the vestry: Andrew Bruce, died 1717.

- Services advertised locally
- Open most days (01957 733242)

SHETLAND

8

SHETLAND

13 ST JOHN'S, BALTASOUND, UNST

**Baltasound
Unst
ZE2 9DX**

⚐ HP 615 088

⛪ Church of Scotland

A968 to Baltasound

Built 1825–7 with local labour at 90°
to the original kirk, the outline of
which is retained in a walled garden.
Much recycled stonework. Significant
alterations in 1959; and reroofed
1984. Hall, kitchen etc. 1990. Original
bell, dated 1828. Pews brought from
Rothiemay, Huntly. Pulpit and
communion table are the work of
Rev. John Firth. Stained glass by
Harry Tait of Trondra, Shetland. Local
war memorials and RAF Saxaford
memorials.

• Sunday: 10.30am
• Open most days (01957 711512)

14 HAROLDSWICK METHODIST CHURCH, UNST

**Haroldswick
Unst
ZE2 9EF**

⚐ HP 646 134

⛪ Methodist

Linked with Lerwick Methodist (4),
East Yell Methodist (20)

On B9087 at Varsgarth

The most northerly church in Britain.
The present building, 1993, was
designed by a Shetland architect,
based on a simplified form of a
Norwegian wooden stave kirk.
Most of the work was done by local
voluntary labour. The interior beams
and panelling are Scandinavian
pine, and the lightness, warmth and
proportion of the worship area are
striking. New bell turret for the 1867
bell erected in 2001.

• Sunday: 11.00am or 6.00pm
  (alternate Sundays)
• Open daily (01595 692874)

15 UYEASOUND KIRK, UNST

**Uyeasound
Unst
ZE2 9DL**

⚔ HP 601 011
⛪ Church of Scotland

From A986, follow signs to Uyeasound and Muness

Built by local people in 1843 at the Disruption. A smaller, and remarkably unaltered, version of Hillside Kirk at Baltasound. The interior is a remarkable survival of wooden pews and pulpit in a balustraded enclosure. An unusual skylight provides natural light to the pulpit. Organ by Solway Organs. Memorials to South Unst men killed in the two World Wars.

- Services advertised locally
- Open most days (01957 755232)

16 ST COLMAN'S EPISCOPAL CHURCH, YELL

**Burravoe
Yell
ZE2 9AY**

⚔ HU 520 798
⛪ Scottish Episcopal

Linked with St Magnus, Lerwick (2)

B9081, 6.5km (4 miles) east of ferry

A little rural gem in Arts & Crafts Gothic. Designed by R. T. N. Spier and built 1900. Apsidal end and spirelet. Herring-bone patterned panels to doors, timber choir stalls and pews. Folding Gothic timber chair by Morris & Co. and painted front to the timber altar depicting the Worship of Heaven.

- Eucharist 2.45pm on two Sundays each month as advertised
- Open daily (01595 693862)

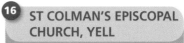

SHETLAND

SHETLAND

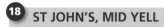

17 ST MAGNUS, HAMNAVOE, YELL

**Hamnavoe
Yell
ZE2 9BA**

⚔ HU 495 804

⛪ Church of Scotland

B9081 from Ulsta ferry

This symmetrical hall-church was built in 1838 on the site of a former church. The gallery was later converted into an upper room. Major refurbishment in 2009, including clear glass windows. The graveyard includes the memorial to the Catalina air crash of 1942. See also the tapestry woven by Mrs Mary Goolden, widow of the pilot.

• Services advertised locally
• Open most days (01957 722231)

B ♿ WC

18 ST JOHN'S, MID YELL

**Mid Yell
Yell
ZE2 9BT**

⚔ HU 515 908

⛪ Church of Scotland

In centre of Mid Yell village

St John's was built around 1832 to a T-plan with two galleries. The seating was reorganised in 1898, remaining unaltered to this day. The high central pulpit with ornate sounding board is the focus of the fine panelled interior of pine with mahogany graining.

• Services advertised locally
• Open most days (01957 702204)

C ♿ WC

19 ST OLAF'S, CULLIVOE, YELL

**Cullivoe
Yell
ZE2 9DD**

HP 544 022

Church of Scotland

Follow B9082 to south of village, overlooking harbour

Harled church built 1832. The unusual crenellated frontage was added in 1886. Two stained-glass memorial windows. Major refurbishment 1988 with new floor and chairs; the pews were retained in the small gallery. New timber ceiling, 2004.

- Services advertised locally
- Open most days (01957 744254)

20 EAST YELL METHODIST CHURCH

**Otterswick
Yell
ZE2 9AU**

HU 517 855

Methodist

Linked with Lerwick Methodist (4), Haroldswick Methodist (14)

B9081, 6.5km (4 miles) north of Burravoe

Built 1892 to serve the needs of the local community, this lovely 'Chapel in the Valley' is noted for its simple beauty, warmth of its welcome and ecumenical nature of its congregation. The chapel has been described as a 'little gem'. Much-admired unique pulpit fall, designed and crafted locally, depicting the Lamb of God.

- Sunday: 10.45am or 2.45pm (alternate Sundays)
- Open daily (01595 692874)

21 ST MAGNUS CATHEDRAL

**Broad Street
Kirkwall
KW15 1DJ**

⚐ HY 449 108

🏛 Church of Scotland

🌐 www.stmagnus.org

The Cathedral Church of St Magnus the Martyr was founded in 1137 by Earl Rognvald Kolson and dedicated to his uncle, Earl Magnus Erlendson. Completed c. 1500, it ranks as one of the finest cathedrals in Scotland. In warm red sandstone, the building is cruciform with a tower over the central crossing. Furnishings of the 1920s in carved oak designed by George Mackie Watson (who also added the copper-clad spire to the tower). Organ by Willis 1926, restored 1971. Owned and maintained by Orkney Islands Council.

- Sunday: 11.15am
- Open April to September, Monday to Saturday 9.00am–6.00pm, Sunday: 1.00–6.00pm; October to March, Monday to Saturday 9.00am–1.00pm and 2.00–5.00pm (01856 874894)

22 KIRKWALL EAST CHURCH

**King Street
Kirkwall
KW15 1NN**

⚐ HY 451 110

🏛 Church of Scotland

🌐 www.orkneycommunities.co.uk/ kirkwalleastchurch

Originally Kirkwall Baptist, built 1892, architect S. Blaikie Jr. Interior reordered in 2002 to provide a functional suite of rooms on two floors for church and community use. Furnishings by Sui Generis, Eday, Orkney. Eustace Ingram organ. The congregation has gained two awards for work with Fairtrade, recycling and use of environmentally friendly products throughout the church.

- Sunday: 11.15am
- Open by arrangement (01856 875469)

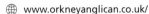

23 ST OLAF'S, KIRKWALL

Dundas Crescent
Kirkwall
KW15 1JQ

⚐ HY 452 106

🏛 Scottish Episcopal

🌐 www.orkneyanglican.co.uk/

Linked with St Mary's, Stromness (29)

St Olaf's was opened by Bishop Suthers on St Olaf's Day (29 July) 1876. It is an imposing building with high timbered ceilings like a ship. Stained glass by Heaton, Butler & Bayne, James Ballantine & Son and Ballantine & Gardiner. Stone credence and aumbry taken from the first St Olaf's of the 9th century. Organ by G. M. Holdich, 1881.

- Sunday: 10.00am
- Open in summer 10.00am–5.00pm; at other times by arrangement (01856 872024)

24 OUR LADY & ST JOSEPH, KIRKWALL

Junction Road
Kirkwall
KW15 1BU

⚐ HY 448 105

🏛 Roman Catholic

Linked with The Italian Chapel, Lambholm (33)

On corner of Main Street

The church is simple but beautiful. A plain dressed-stone chapel of 1877 with priest's house attached, it features a set of wooden Stations of the Cross by Marvin Elliott.

- Sunday: Mass 5.00pm; Monday: Mass 12.00 noon; Tuesday to Saturday: communion service 12.00 noon
- Open daily 10.00am–5.00pm (01856 771495)

25 ST MAGNUS, BIRSAY

**Birsay
KW17 2LX**

⚑ HY 248 277

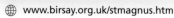 Non-denominational

🌐 www.birsay.org.uk/stmagnus.htm

Across the road from the Earl's Palace

The original church was built by Earl Thorfinn c. 1060 and has been altered and restored several times, most recently in 1986. Stained-glass window by Alex Strachan showing scenes from the life of St Magnus. Inside the church are two 16th- and 17th-century tombstones. The Mons Bellus stone is probably from the nearby Bishop's Palace. Maintained by the St Magnus Church Birsay Trust.

- Occasional services
- Key available at Palace Stores (01856 721241)

   (toilets near car park)

26 EAST MAINLAND CHURCH

**Holm
KW17 2SB**

⚑ HY 504 019

 Church of Scotland

3km (2 miles) east of St Mary's on B9052

Overlooking Holm Sound, Lambholm and the Churchill Barriers, Holm Parish Church was originally built as an Antiburgher Meeting House in 1814. The church was largely rebuilt in the 1920s after a fire. A large, simple building with grey-harled walls and a hipped gabled roof. Plans are under way for a major refurbishment.

- Sunday: 11.00am
- Open by arrangement (01856 861311)

27 ST MICHAEL'S, HARRAY

Harray
KW17 2LD

⚘ HY 314 179

🏛 Church of Scotland

A986, between Finstown and Dounby

Plain white rendered church of
1836 with Caithness slate roof and
round-headed windows. Pulpit
with sounding board with pews
and galleries round three sides. Five
stained-glass windows. Refurbished
1980s; and extension of 1984 houses
the vestry, meeting room, kitchen and
toilets. The bell, dated 1724, was gifted
by the Earl of Morton.

- Sunday: 11.00am
- Open by arrangement (01856 771803)

28 ST PETER'S, SANDWICK

Skaill Kirk

Sandwick
KW16 3LS

⚘ HY 235 199

🏛 Former Church of Scotland

🌐 www.srct.org.uk

1.6km (1 mile) north of Skara Brae

A rare survival of a quite exceptional
unaltered Scots parish kirk of 1836.
Situated on a rugged and exposed
site, commanding views over the Bay
of Skaill. Dominated by a towering
pulpit reaching to gallery height, the
austere interior powerfully evokes the
experience of Presbyterian worship
in the 19th century when over 500
packed the building – each allowed
a mere 18 inches of pew. Acquired by
the Scottish Redundant Churches
Trust in 1998 and restored in 2002–3.

- Occasional services
- Open April to October 10.00am–
  6.00pm; November to March by
  arrangement (01334 472032)

ORKNEY

29 ST MARY'S, STROMNESS

**Church Road
Stromness
KW16 3BA**

⚑ HY 253 091

⛪ Scottish Episcopal

🌐 www.orkneyanglican.co.uk/

Linked with St Olaf's, Kirkwall (23)

Established as a mission church in July 1885, St Mary's became an independent charge, moving into the present building, in 1888. The font and ciborium were given by the Earl of Zetland. Joined with St Olaf's in Kirkwall in 1943. Two beautiful modern stained-glass windows.

- Sunday: 11.30am; Thursday: 11.00am
- Open by arrangement (01856 872024)

30 ST COLUMBA'S, LONGHOPE, HOY

**Longhope
Hoy
KW16 3PA**

⚑ ND 312 908

⛪ Church of Scotland

Built 1832 with windows on the south wall, and the pulpit in the middle of the wall. Pews and gallery on three sides of the pulpit. Communion table of carved oak by local tradesmen, gifted by the Guild, 1924. Sandstone font sculpted by a local mason to a design by W. R. Lethaby, architect of Melsetter House. Panels above vestry from the Spanish Armada.

- Sunday: 11.15am
- Open daily (entry through vestry door) (01856 701363)

31 ST JOHN'S TRUST CHURCH, NORTH WALLS, HOY

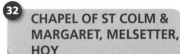

**Lyness
Hoy
KW16 3NX**

ND 297 916

Non-denominational

On B9047, 3km (2 miles) south of Lyness

A mission kirk, built in 1883 as a counter-attraction to the nearby Free kirk. It was built by public subscription and often referred to as 'the Fisher Kirk', owing to the esteem in which its longest-serving missionary, Mr Fisher, was held. Except for gas heating, all the fittings (pews, oil lamps etc.) are original.

- Services by arrangement
- Open daily (01856 791248)

32 CHAPEL OF ST COLM & MARGARET, MELSETTER, HOY

**Melsetter
Hoy
KW16 3NZ**

ND 270 893

Ecumenical

On B9047 at south end of Hoy

Originally the Episcopal chapel for Melsetter House, William Richard Lethaby's Arts & Crafts 1900 masterwork. The chapel was his first experiment with concrete as a structural material. The theme for the chapel draws on the resonance between ship and church in the early days of Christianity (Hebrews 6:19). Stained glass by Morris, Whall and Burne-Jones. Hanging by William Morris.

- Occasional services
- Open by arrangement (01856 791352)

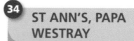

33 THE ITALIAN CHAPEL, LAMBHOLM

Lambholm
KW17 2RT

🏹 HY 488 006

⛪ Roman Catholic

🌐 www.catholicchurchorkney.org.uk

Linked with Our Lady, Kirkwall (24)

All that remains of the Italian prisoner-of-war Camp 60, the famous Italian Chapel was created from two Nissen huts in 1943–4, using material from sunken blockships in Scapa Flow. Wonderful testimony to the artistic skills of Domenico Chiocchetti and his fellow prisoners. Beautifully designed chancel, altar, altar-rail and holy water stoup. Painted glass windows depicting St Francis of Assisi and St Catherine of Siena. Restored 1960.

- 3.30pm on 1st Sunday of summer months
- Open daily (01856 872462)

34 ST ANN'S, PAPA WESTRAY

Holland
Papa Westray
KW17 2BU

🏹 HY 495 516

⛪ Church of Scotland

Linked with Westray (40)

Next to school in centre of island

Built in 1841, this was the first church in Scotland to be given to the Free Church by the proprietor. Rectangular building with rubble masonry walls and harled exterior. Restored 2001 by Orkney Islands Council, Health Board and congregation, St Ann's is now home to the island's surgery, a small flat and community facilities. Several beautiful locally made felt hangings.

- Sunday: 2.30pm
- Open daily (01857 644221)

(by arrangement)

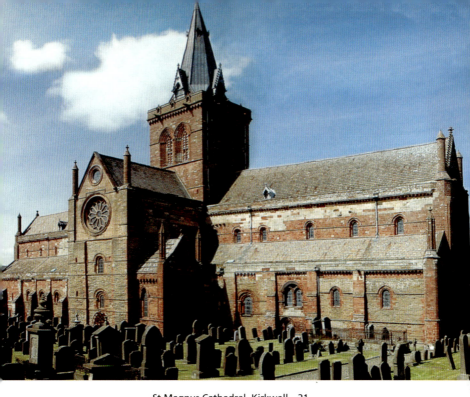

St Magnus Cathedral, Kirkwall   21

St Olaf's, Kirkwall   23

Cawdor Parish Church   88

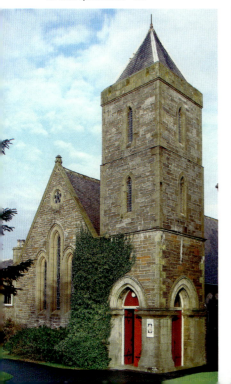

Halkirk & Westerdale Parish Church   43

Applecross Church   65

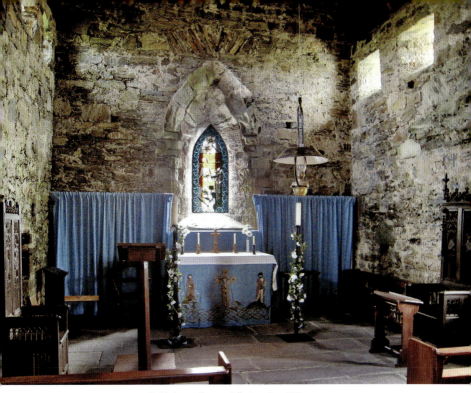

St Moluag, Eoropaidh, Lewis   136

St Andrew's Cathedral, Inverness   99

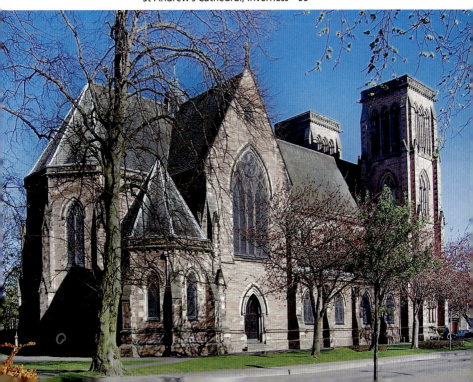

St Michael & All Angels, Inverness   101

St Duthac's, Dornie   72

The Italian Chapel, Lambholm   33

Westray Parish Kirk   40

St Maelrubha's, Poolewe   82

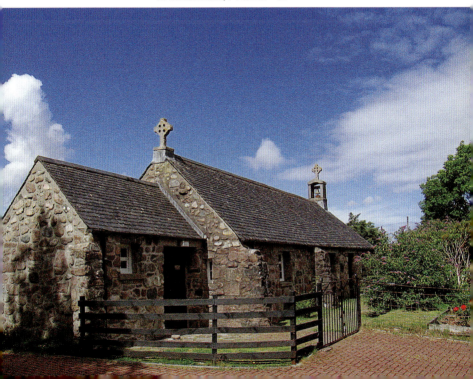

St Boniface, Papa Westray   35

Clachan Church, Applecross   66

St Magnus, Birsay   25

Melness Church   58

St Peter's, Sandwick   28

St Columba's (Old Parish) Church, Stornoway   137

35 ST BONIFACE, PAPA WESTRAY

**Papa Westray
KW17 2BU**

HY 488 527

Non-denominational

On west coast of island

Two Pictish cross-slabs found in the kirkyard (one now in Orkney Museum, Kirkwall, the other in NMS) indicate that there was an 8th-century church here. The present building dates from the 12th century, enlarged early 1700s and furnished with box pews, gallery and high pulpit. Restored 1993. Norse period hog-backed tombstone in the kirkyard.

- Occasional services
- Open daily (01857 644250)

36 OLD ST MARY'S, BURWICK, SOUTH RONALDSAY

**Burwick
South Ronaldsay
KW17 2RW**

ND 441 843

Church of Scotland

Close to ferry pier

Built on what is often claimed to be the earliest Christian site in Orkney, the former South Kirk was erected in 1599. The present building, set in a small graveyard, overlooking the Ayre of Burwick, was constructed in 1790. The interior was renovated in 1860. Contains what is now believed to be a Pictish coronation stone.

- No regular services
- Open by arrangement (01856 831212)

ORKNEY

ORKNEY

37 ST PETER'S, SOUTH RONALDSAY

**Eastside
South Ronaldsay
KW17 2TJ**

ND 471 908

Church of Scotland

On east coast of island

Formerly the North Parish Church for the island, the present oblong harled building, with Caithness slates in its churchyard, was constructed in the 17th century and renovated in 1801 and 1967. Features a pulpit with sounding board on the long wall and a long central communion table (believed to be unique in Orkney). All pews are thought to be made from driftwood. The oil lamps have been converted to electricity.

- Sunday: 11.00am (June and August only)
- Open by arrangement (01856 831706)

38 ST MARGARET'S, SOUTH RONALDSAY

**Church Road
St Margaret's Hope
South Ronaldsay
KW17 2SR**

ND 449 936

Church of Scotland

Opened 1856 by the United Presbyterian Church and enlarged 1870. Its central location in the village of St Margaret's Hope led to its being designated as the principal place of worship for the parish of South Ronaldsay and Burray. Communion table and font from former St Lawrence's Church, Burray.

- Sunday: 11.00am (except June and August)
- Open by arrangement (01856 831251)

ORKNEY

39 MONCUR MEMORIAL CHURCH, STRONSAY

Wardhill
Stronsay
KW17 2AG

⚡ HY 654 252

⛪ Church of Scotland

By junction of B9060 and B9061

Stronsay's only church, built in 1955 to a design by Leslie Grahame MacDougall. A large, harled, cruciform building, retaining many traditional Orcadian features in its construction. Red sandstone and blue whinstone blend with the wooden floor and large roof trusses to give a quiet, dignified appearance. Beautiful stained-glass window of 'Christ as the Good Shepherd' by Marjorie Kemp, 1935.

- Sunday: 11.00am
- Open daily 9.00am–9.00pm May to September; at other times by arrangement (01857 616322)

40 WESTRAY PARISH KIRK

Kirkbrae
Westray
KW17 2DB

⚡ HY 457 462

⛪ Church of Scotland

Linked with Papa Westray (34)

B9066, 3km (2 miles) south-east of Pierowall

Oblong barn-like building, built 1846, with part-piended roof of local flagstone slates. Original pulpit with canopy, topped by a dove. Whole building refurbished in 2002–3. Renewable energy (ground-source heat pump and wind turbine) to meet energy needs. Pipe organ by Solway Organs, 1967.

- Sunday: 11.30am; evening services shared with Baptist and United Free Kirks
- Open daily (01857 677357)

41 **BOWER CHURCH OF SCOTLAND**

Bower
KW1 4TT

ND 238 622

Church of Scotland

www.centralcaithnesschurches.org

Linked with Halkirk & Westerdale (43)

Midway between Thurso and Wick on B876

Built 1847, architect William Davidson, altered 1902 by architect Donald Leed. Finialled and panelled Gothic screen flanks pulpit. Unusual in that the pulpit is in the north, not south, wall. Stained-glass window dedicated to Sir John Sinclair, 7th Baronet of Dunbeath. Mural memorials to members of Henderson and Sinclair families; and plaque in memory of Zachary Pont, minister 1605–13, and his wife Margaret, daughter of John Knox.

Sunday: 12.15pm
Open by arrangement (01955 621220)

42 **CANISBAY CHURCH**

Canisbay
KW1 4YB

ND 343 728

Church of Scotland

www.canisbaychurch.org

Kirkstyle, on A836

Most northerly place of worship on the Scottish mainland, the site was occupied by the Chapel of St Drostan, who headed a mission to Pictland in the 6th century. The present cruciform church is largely 17th-century, but the nave incorporates walling from the medieval church and a worn 17th-century monument flanked by pairs of Corinthian pilasters. West tower added 1704. John de Groat stone of 1568 stands in the vestibule.

- Sunday: 12.00 noon
- Open daily 9.00am–9.00pm, Easter to end October (01955 611756)

43 HALKIRK & WESTERDALE PARISH CHURCH

**Bridge Street
Halkirk
KW12 6YG**

ND 130 585

Church of Scotland

Linked with Bower (41)

At south end of main street

Rectangular church with Italian Romanesque west gable façade, completed 1886, designed by the Inverness architect Alexander Ross. It was built as a Free Church, became United Free in 1900 and Church of Scotland in 1935. Original fittings in interior, including panelled gallery and raised minister's desk.

- Sunday: 10.00am
- Open by arrangement (01955 621220)

44 THRUMSTER PARISH CHURCH

**Thrumster
KW1 5TX**

ND 333 447

Church of Scotland

At junction of A9 with road to Tannoch

This attractive church was built in 1910 after a large number of local residents signed a petition calling for a church to be built in the area. Notable for its very pleasing decor, stained-glass window and exceptional acoustics.

- Sunday: 3.00pm
- Open by arrangement (01955 651711)

45 ST PETER'S & ST ANDREW'S CHURCH, THURSO

Princess Street
Thurso
KW14 7BQ

ND 116 684

Church of Scotland

http://users.ecosse.net/spandsacos/

Built in 1832 to a design by William Burn, the church is the centre point of the town, fronted by the town square garden and war memorial. Substantial Gothic building with buttressed walls and a tall square tower. Impressive U-plan gallery. Pipe organ, Norman & Beard, 1914. Stained glass includes 'The Sower' by Oscar Paterson, 1922.

- 11.00am each Sunday, and 6.30pm on 1st Sunday of the month
- Open by arrangement (01847 894441)

46 ST PETER & THE HOLY ROOD, THURSO

Thurso Episcopal Church

Sir George's Street
Thurso
KW14 7AW

ND 117 682

Scottish Episcopal

Linked with St John's, Wick (48)

The church was built in 1883–4 to the design of Alexander Ross, the chancel being added in 1905 in memory of Mr Norman Sinclair. The stained glass by A. L. Moore depicting 'The Good Samaritan' is in memory of Sir George Sinclair of Ulbster. The 2-manual organ by George Benson, 1894, built for a Lancashire chapel, was dismantled and moved here in 1973. The carved oak reredos depicts the Ascension and the first Pentecost.

- Sunday: 8.00am, 9.30am and 6.30pm; Tuesday: 10.30am; Friday: 7.00pm
- By arrangement (01847 893393)

HIGHLAND

CAITHNESS

47 PULTENEYTOWN PARISH CHURCH, WICK

**Argyle Square
Wick
KW1 5AJ**

Ⓐ ND 365 505

♫ Church of Scotland

⊕ www.pulteneytownchurch.org.uk

Built in 1842 as the centrepiece of Thomas Telford's Argyle Square in the new settlement of Pulteneytown, which was commissioned by the British Fisheries Society for the rapidly expanding population of Wick. Designed by local architect Davidson, the interior has an all-round gallery. Completely renovated 2004.

- Sunday: 11.30am and 6.30pm
- Open Wednesday and Saturday 10.00am–12.00 noon or by arrangement (01955 603166)

   (on Sundays)

 (Wed and Sat 10.00am–12.00 noon)

48 ST JOHN THE EVANGELIST, WICK

**Moray Street
Wick
KW1 5QF**

Ⓐ ND 363 505

♫ Scottish Episcopal

⊕ www.stjohnswick.org.uk/

Linked with St Peter's, Thurso (46)

Junction with Francis Street

Built in 1870 to a design by Alexander Ross of Inverness, St John's is especially attractive, with a warm friendly atmosphere. Four-light windows known affectionately as the 'I am' windows ('I am the Good Shepherd', 'the Resurrection and the Life', 'the True Vine', 'the Bread of Life'), by David Gulland, a former member of the vestry of St John's.

- Sunday: 11.30am; first Wednesday of each month: 10.30am
- Open by arrangement (01955 609291)

   (in halls)

ALTNAHARRA PARISH CHURCH

Altnaharra
IV27 4UG

NC 568 355

Church of Scotland

Linked with Farr (50), Strathnaver (63)

A836, west end of Loch Naver

Halfway between the school and the Telford bridge, the church was built 1854–7 by Hugh Mackay as a Free church. Fine stonework and interior woodwork. Oil lamps now converted to electricity. Long communion tables between front pews for communicants to sit at. Stained-glass window in memory of Kathleen Joan Kimball.

- No regular services
- Open daily (01549 402373)

 ## FARR PARISH CHURCH, BETTYHILL

Bettyhill
KW14 7SS

NC 708 622

Church of Scotland

Linked with Altnaharra (49), Strathnaver (63)

North of A836

Built by Sinclair MacDonald in 1909 to a standard design used for United Free churches in the Highlands. Nearby, at Clachan, stands the old parish church, built 1774, now a museum of the Clearances and Clan Mackay. Among the gravestones is the Farr Stone, a Christianised Pictish stone. The Strathnaver Trail runs from the museum to Altnaharra.

- Sunday: 11.30am
- Open daily (01641 521208)

51 CROICK CHURCH

Croick
IV24 3BS

⚓ NH 457 915

⛪ Church of Scotland

Linked with Edderton (54)

16km (10 miles) west of Ardgay, 1.6km (1 mile) west of junction at Amat Lodge

Harled T-plan 'Parliamentary' church built by James Smith, 1827, from a Thomas Telford design. One of the few Parliamentary churches still in use in its original form. Furnishings virtually unchanged since first built; old-style long communion table and original pulpit. East window has messages scratched in 1845 by evicted inhabitants of Glen Calvie.

- 3.00pm, 2nd Sunday of the month, May to September
- Open during daylight hours (01863 766285)

52 DORNOCH CATHEDRAL

High Street
Dornoch
IV25 3HP

⚓ NH 797 897

⛪ Church of Scotland

🌐 www.dornoch-cathedral.com

Cathedral founded by Bishop Gilbert de Moravia in the 13th century; the first service in the building was held in 1239. The medieval masonry of the chancel and the crossing piers remains mostly intact today. The nave was destroyed by fire in 1570, the transepts and choir were reroofed 1616, and the nave rebuilt 1837. In 1924, the interior stonework was exposed. Lavish display of stained glass, including several windows by James Ballantine, others by Percy Bacon, and the St Gilbert window by Crear McCartney, 1989.

- Sunday: all year 11.00am, and summer months 8.30pm
- Open during daylight hours (01862 810296)

53 ST FINNBARR'S, DORNOCH

**Schoolhill
Dornoch
IV25 3PF**

A NH 799 898

🏰 Scottish Episcopal

Simple but picturesque Gothic church by Alexander Ross, 1912–13. Stained-glass triple-lancet east window by Percy Bacon. Of special note are the 70 tapestry kneelers with Highland themes created by 14 members of the congregation between 1981 and 1993.

- 1st and 3rd Sunday of the month: 9.45am; 2nd and 4th Sunday of the month: 11.30am; 5th Sunday: varies, check with vestry secretary
- Open April to October 10.00am– 4.00pm; or by arrangement (01862 810243)

54 EDDERTON OLD PARISH CHURCH

**Edderton
IV19 1JY**

A NH 719 843

🏰 Church of Scotland

Linked with Croick (51)

East end of Edderton village

Remarkably intact example of a mid-18th-century church, built 1743 on a much older site. Long, low, harled building with rectangular windows and piended dormers. Galleried interior with two-tier pulpit, elders' pews, and front pews with fold-down backs to form long communion tables. Pictish symbol stone in churchyard. Superb 19th-century preaching 'ark' in adjacent new burial ground.

- Occasional services
- Open by arrangement (01863 766285)

55 ST ANDREW'S PARISH CHURCH, GOLSPIE

**Main Street
Golspie
KW10 6RH**

NC 838 002

Church of Scotland

www.standrewsgolspie.com/

On A9 at north end of village

The Earl of Sutherland's chapel, recorded in the 13th century, became the parish church in 1619. The present cruciform building was constructed 1736–7 and extended 1751 with only minor changes since. Superb carved pulpit and earl's loft, 1737–9, by Kenneth Sutherland, the joiner at Dunrobin. Replica pews by George Hay, 1953. Described by John Gifford in the *Pevsner Buildings of Scotland* as 'the epitome of the Georgian parish kirk'.

- Sunday: 11.00am all year, except last Sunday of the month April to September, when service is in Fountain Road Hall
- Open by arrangement (01408 633295)

56 HALLADALE PARISH CHURCH

**Craigtown
KW13 6YU**

NC 893 558

Church of Scotland

www.northcoastparishchurch.org

Linked with Reay (59), Strathy (62)

On A897, 11km (7 miles) south of Melvich, Strath Halladale

The church for the scattered community of Strath Halladale. Combined church and manse of 1910, built in corrugated iron with timber detailing. Probably by Speirs of Glasgow and transported by railway to Forsinard, 8 miles to the south.

- 11.00am, 5th Sunday of the month (where applicable)
- Open by arrangement (01847 811441)

1

HIGHLAND

SUTHERLAND

57 LAIRG PARISH CHURCH

Church Hill Road
Lairg
IV27 4BL

NC 583 065

Church of Scotland,
Scottish Episcopal

Church of Scotland congregation linked with Pitfure, Rogart (60), St Callan's, Rogart (61)

A simple Gothic church, built of local granite 1847, designed by William Leslie. Renovated 2001. The graveyard, 1½ miles away, served the original church and contains some interesting monuments, including a large marble monument to Sir James Matheson of Achany.

- Church of Scotland: 10.45am every Sunday, and 6.30pm on 1st Sunday of the month; Scottish Episcopal: Sunday 8.30am
- Open by arrangement (01549 402373)

58 MELNESS CHURCH

Melness
IV27 4YS

NC 586 634

Church of Scotland

Linked with St Andrew's, Tongue (64)

Near Talmine, 6.5km (4 miles) from junction with A838

Built at the turn of the 20th century by local craftsmen to replace an earlier building at an adjacent site. Interior totally wood-lined. Local feeling was that it should have been called the 'Kerr Memorial Church', as it was due to the minister at the time, Rev. Cathel Kerr, that the church was completed.

- Sunday: 12.30pm
- Open at all times

59 REAY PARISH CHURCH

**Reay
KW14 7RG**

NC 967 648

Church of Scotland

www.northcoastparishchurch.org

Linked with Halladale (56), Strathy (62)

On A836 at east end of village

Overlooking Sandside Bay, a white-harled T-plan church of 1738–9 with a pyramid-roofed bell-tower at the east end. Traditional layout inside with a long central communion table and a hexagonal pulpit with sounding board. The nearby old churchyard contains several notable monuments, including the mausoleum of the Mackays of Bighouse of 1691.

- 11.00am, 1st and 3rd Sunday of the month
- Open by arrangement (01847 811441)

60 PITFURE CHURCH, ROGART

Parish of Rogart

**Rogart
IV28 3UA**

NC 710 038

Church of Scotland

Linked with Lairg (57), St Callan's, Rogart (61)

On A839

A simple, pleasant place in which to worship. Built by the United Free congregation in 1910, architect Robert J. Macbeth, Inverness.

- 12.15pm on 1st, 3rd and 5th Sunday of the month, and 6.30pm on 2nd Sunday of the month
- Open by arrangement (01408 642224)

HIGHLAND

SUTHERLAND

61 ST CALLAN'S, ROGART

Rogart
IV28 3XE

NC 715 038
Church of Scotland

Linked with Lairg (57), Pitfure, Rogart (60)

On A839

Rebuilt in 1777 on the site of a medieval church. The austere whitewashed exterior with its plain sash windows gives little hint of the warm, gleaming interior. A high canopied pulpit stands against the east wall. Long communion table and pews. Other pews are tiered from the entrance to the west end. Two small stained-glass windows by Margaret Chilton and Marjorie Kemp, 1929. Modern vestry wing built in 1984.

- September to June: 12.15pm on 2nd and 4th Sunday of the month
- Open daily, Easter to end October; other times by arrangement (01408 642224)

62 STRATHY PARISH CHURCH

Strathy
KW14 7RY

NC 830 657
Church of Scotland
www.northcoastparishchurch.org

Linked with Halladale (56), Reay (59)

On A836 at junction with road to Strathy Point

Originally built in 1910 for the United Free Church, probably by R. J. Macbeth. A simple hall-church of stone with a slate roof and gableted bellcote, and with a five-light window over the door.

- 11.00am, 2nd and 4th Sunday of the month
- Open by arrangement (01847 811441)

Gaelic

63 STRATHNAVER PARISH CHURCH, SYRE

Syre Church

**Syre
KW11 6UA**

NC 694 439

Church of Scotland

Linked with Altnaharra (49), Farr (50)

Junction of B871 and B873

Built 1901 as a mission station from Altnaharra. Pre-fabricated by Speirs & Co., Glasgow, and erected on site. Neat and tiny corrugated-iron church lined with wood. Plaque in memory of Rev. Robert Sloan, minister 1969–74. Modern cemetery and car park across the road. Nearby is the Rossal clearance village, maintained by the Forestry Commission, and Patrick Sellar's house.

- 3.00pm on 2nd, 4th and 5th Sunday of the month
- Open daily (01641 521208)

64 ST ANDREW'S, TONGUE

**Tongue
IV27 4XF**

NC 591 570

Church of Scotland

Linked with Melness (58)

On A838 Durness road, past Tongue Hotel

Rebuilt by Donald Mackay, Master of Reay, in 1680 following the Reay family's conversion to Protestantism (c. 1600). The site was that of the ancient Celtic and latterly Roman Catholic Church (St Peter's Chapel). During a renovation in 1729, a vault was built covering the graves of earlier members of the Mackay family.

- Sunday: 11.00am
- Open at all times

65 APPLECROSS CHURCH

**Camusterrach
Applecross
IV54 8LU**

NG 711 417

Church of Scotland

Linked with Lochcarron (78)

3km (2 miles) towards Toscaig from post office

Plain harled church built in 1855 for the Free Church. Became United Free Church in 1900 and Church of Scotland in 1929. Clachan Church at the head of Applecross Bay is also open to visitors. Applecross has connections with the 7th-century St Maelrubha.

- Sunday: 1.00pm
- Open by arrangement (01520 744248)

66 CLACHAN CHURCH, APPLECROSS

**Applecross
IV54 8ND**

NG 714 458

Inter-denominational

www.applecross.org.uk

North side of Applecross Bay

Standing on the ancient site of St Maelrubha's church (AD 673), the present church was built in 1817. An incised Celtic cross by the gate is said to mark the grave of Ruairidh Mor MacAogan, abbot of Applecross, who died in AD 801. Remains of carved Celtic crosses, dating from the 8th century, in heritage centre opposite. The beauty and tranquillity of the surroundings complement the quiet simplicity of the plain stone building, a fitting heritor of the old Gaelic name of A' *Chomraich* – the Sanctuary.

- No regular services
- Open daily (01463 715961)

67 AVOCH PARISH CHURCH

**Braehead
Avoch
IV9 8QL**

NH 702 552

Church of Scotland

www.avochchurch.co.uk

**Linked with Fortrose (74),
Rosemarkie (84)**

Take Killen Road up the hill from
hotel

Gothic Revival-style church with
prominent spire by Alexander Ross,
completed 1872. Vestry contains a late
medieval decorative aumbry c. 1500.
Small pipe organ by Miller of Dundee.
Stained-glass windows in east and
west gables by Henry M. Barnett of
Newcastle. Three wall hangings by
Mrs Lilian Noble of Avoch and two
others by ladies of Avoch Church
Guild. Sir Alexander Mackenzie of
Canada is buried in the graveyard.

- Sunday: 10.00am
- Open by arrangement (01381 620043)

68 CONTIN PARISH CHURCH

Contin Kirk

**Contin
IV14 9ES**

NH 456 558

Church of Scotland

Linked with Lochluichart (79)

At east end of village, signposted
between line of houses

A pre-Reformation church founded by
St Maelrubha in AD 690 on an island,
Abhainn Dubh, in the Blackwater.
The church had to be rebuilt after the
MacDonalds burnt the church and
congregation in 1477. Major repairs
1734; reroofed and the bellcote added
1760. The walls were heightened by
eight feet in 1832 and two galleries
installed; only the east gallery
survives following the reordering of
the interior in 1919. Stained glass by
Roland Mitton. Two late medieval
grave-slabs in the vestibule.

- Sunday: 10.45am
- Open by arrangement (01997 423296)

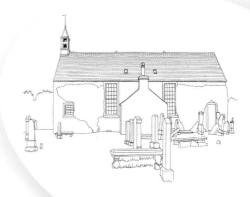

69 EAST CHURCH, CROMARTY

**Church Street
Cromarty
IV11 8XA**

NH 791 673

Former Church of Scotland

www.eastchurchcromarty.co.uk/

Described by John Hume as 'unquestionably one of the finest 18th-century parish churches in Scotland', starting as a simple east–west rectangle in medieval times. The north aisle was added in 1739 to create a T-plan church. Further alterations in 1756 and 1798. The interior dates principally from the 18th century, with galleries added to accommodate the growing congregation, the most elaborate being the Cromartie loft of 1756. Several fine monuments. Owned and maintained by the Scottish Redundant Churches Trust.

- Occasional services
- Open daily (01334 472032)

70 DINGWALL OLD PARISH CHURCH

St Clement's

**Church Street
Dingwall
IV15 9PB**

NH 549 589

Church of Scotland

www.saint-clements.org

Junction with Tulloch Street

Hall-church with semi-octagonal gallery, built 1799–1803 by George Burn, 'urbane, but isolated in its churchyard'. Four large Gothic windows on the south side; classical pediment on the north side topped with octagonal tower and spire. Interior altered 1875 by William C. Joass; Jacobean-style pulpit with sounding board. Stained glass by James Steel & Co. and Abbey Studio.

- Sunday: 11.30am September to May, 9.15am (in hall) June, July and August
- Open by arrangement (01349 863063)

   (in halls)

71 ST JAMES THE GREAT, DINGWALL

Castle Street
Dingwall
IV15 9HU

A NH 552 588

🏠 Scottish Episcopal

🌐 www.stjames-stannes.org.uk

Linked with St Anne's, Strathpeffer (86)

The building is on the site of an earlier chapel, 1806, which was demolished in 1851 and the new simple and compact building erected to a new Gothic design by J. L. Pearson. It was consecrated in 1854 but gutted by fire in 1871. Restoration, by Alexander Ross, Inverness, began immediately, following the original design. New halls added 2005.

- Sunday: 9.30am or 11.00am, alternating with St Anne's, Strathpeffer; Wednesday: 10.30am (please check notice-board for details)
- Open daily during daylight hours (01349 862204)

72 ST DUTHAC'S, DORNIE

Dornie
IV40 8EL

A NG 884 268

🏠 Roman Catholic

🌐 www.spanglefish.com/
stduthacsdornie

Beside Eilean Donan Castle

The first Catholic church on the site was built in 1703. The present building dates from 1860, architect Joseph A. Hansom. It is in simple Gothic style with nave and chancel. The stone reredos has polished granite shafts, while similar columns support the altar. The simplicity continues with the semi-octagonal stone pulpit and braced-rafter roof.

- Saturday: 7.30pm; Sunday: 10.30am
- Open daily (01599 555229)

73 FEARN ABBEY

Hill of Fearn
by Tain
IV20 1SS

NH 837 773

Church of Scotland

Linked with Tarbat (Portmahomack) (83)

West of B9166, just outside Hill of Fearn heading south

Known as 'the Lamp of the North', it is one of the oldest pre-Reformation Scottish churches still in use for worship. Rebuilt 1772 by James Rich and restored by Ian G. Lindsay & Partners, 1972. Further restoration in summer 2001. Originally a monastery of Premonstratensian monks of the Order of St Augustine. Patrick Hamilton, burnt for heresy at St Andrews in 1528, was the Commendatory Abbot from 1517 to 1528.

- Sunday: 11.30am
- Open daily April to September, 10.00am–4.00pm; or by arrangement (01862 832626)

 74 FORTROSE PARISH CHURCH

High Street
Fortrose
IV10 8TF

NH 728 568

Church of Scotland

www.fortrosemarkiechurchof scotland.org

Linked with Avoch (67), Rosemarkie (84)

A832

Close to the ruined medieval Chanonry Cathedral, this handsome Gothic Revival edifice with its tall spire was completed in 1898 for the Free Church by John Robertson. The interior has a fine hammer-beam roof, pitch-pine galleries and elaborate and imposing pulpit. The congregation united with Rosemarkie in 1967, and services alternate between the two church buildings.

- Sunday: 11.30am in January, March, May, July, September and November, 6.00pm in other months
- Open by arrangement (01381 620381)

75 GAIRLOCH FREE CHURCH

**Gairloch
IV21 2BH**

NG 805 760

Free Church of Scotland

A832, 1.6km (1 mile) south of Gairloch

Stone-built church with a slate roof on a commanding site overlooking Loch Gairloch and the Torridon mountains. Gothic in style with a nave and short transepts, to a design by Matthews & Lawrie, 1878. The entrance façade is topped with pinnacles and belfry. Simple interior with original fittings and Gothic panelled gallery across east end.

- Sunday: 11.00am and 5.00pm; Gaelic Service: 12.00 noon alternate Sundays
- Open by arrangement (01445 741239)

76 INVER MEETING HOUSE

**New Street
Inver
IV20 1RX**

NH 863 828

Church of Scotland

10km (6 miles) east of Tain

A Meeting House in the style of cottages. Inver, still largely in its original form, originated as a settlement of persons displaced during the Clearances. A memorial, to the north of the village on the shore, marks the common grave of cholera victims, a large proportion of the population.

- 6.00pm on 2nd and 4th Sunday of the month
- Open by arrangement (01862 871522)

HIGHLAND

ROSS & CROMARTY

77 ST DONNAN'S CHURCH, LOCHALSH

Nostie
IV40 8EQ

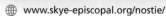

NG 855 272

Scottish Episcopal

www.skye-episcopal.org/nostie/

1.6km (1 mile) east of Auchtertyre, on A87

St Donnan was a friend and disciple of St Columba. Unassuming, simple church by Stevenson & Dunworth, 1962–4. East wall inside is patterned with panels inset with stones from the Nostie Burn. The angels on the altar pedestal were carved by F. R. Stevenson.

• Sunday: 10.30am
• If church is locked, key obtainable from Fernfield, Nostie (opposite the church) (01470 521271)

78 LOCHCARRON PARISH CHURCH

West Church

Lochcarron
IV54 8YB

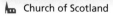

NG 894 392

Church of Scotland

Linked with Applecross (65)

Centre of Lochcarron, off A896

Former United Free Church designed by William Mackenzie, 1910. Crisply painted; standard UF layout. Also of interest is the burial ground 1.6km (1 mile) east of the village.

• Sunday: 10.30am; Wednesday: 7.30pm
• Open daily in summer months (01520 722829)

79 LOCHLUICHART PARISH CHURCH

**Lochluichart
IV23 2PZ**

NH 317 626

Church of Scotland

Linked with Contin (68)

On A832, 800 metres (½ mile) west of Lochluichart Station

A T-plan Parliamentary church built 1825–7 (at a cost of £1,689 3s 3d!) to Thomas Telford's standard design. The interior has since been reordered and the original doors blocked. In the graveyard, there is a large table monument to Louisa, Lady Ashburton of Rosehall.

- Sunday: 12.15pm
- Open by arrangement (01997 423296)

80 OUR LADY & ST BEAN, MARYDALE

**Marydale
IV4 7LT**

NH 342 317

Roman Catholic

Linked with St Mary's, Beauly (91), St Mary's, Eskadale (95)

North side of A831, between Cannich Bridge and Comar Bridge

Simple stone church in Gothic style, with adjoining presbytery, walled garden, school and schoolhouse, built as a unit by Joseph A. Hansom, 1868. On the other side of the road is Clachan Comair, a walled graveyard with the ruins of a small 17th-century church, on the site of an early 10th-century chapel dedicated to St Bean. In 1998, a new altar was made from 300-year-old oak, designed by local artist Alistair MacPherson.

- Sunday: 9.00am
- Open daily (01463 233519)

HIGHLAND

ROSS & CROMARTY

HIGHLAND

ROSS & CROMARTY

81 NIGG OLD CHURCH

**Nigg
IV19 1QR**

🏹 NH 805 717

🏛 Church of Scotland

🌐 www.niggoldtrust.org.uk

On south-west approach to village of Nigg

The earliest recording is 1255/6, when the parson had to swear allegiance to Edward I of England. Medieval structure largely rebuilt 1626 and again in 1723–5, with alterations 1779–84. The north aisle and belfry were added in 1730–1. Church closed for worship in 1990 and now cared for by Nigg Old Trust. Important late 8th-century cross-slab moved indoors in 1978. On the Pictish Trail. Beautiful and historic Bishop's Walk immediately adjacent to the church.

- Occasional services
- Open 10.00am–5.00pm, daily April to October or by arrangement with Nigg Old Trust (01862 851222)

82 ST MAELRUBHA'S, POOLEWE

**St Maelrubha's Close
Poolewe
IV26 2XE**

🏹 NG 857 807

🏛 Scottish Episcopal

🌐 www.spanglefish.com/
stmaelrubhapoolewe/

In centre of village

The first Episcopal church to be built on the north-west coast of Scotland since the Jacobite Rebellion of 1745, St Maelrubha's (a former cow byre) was dedicated in 1965. Tiny, simple and made of local stone, it houses a fragment of the Celtic cross erected as a monument to the saint and brought from Applecross. Memorial to the Highland Fieldcraft Training Centre.

- Sunday: 11.00am; 5.30pm on 1st Wednesday of the month; 10.30am on all other Wednesdays
- Open during daylight hours (01445 712176)

 (in church hall)

83 TARBAT CHURCH (PORTMAHOMACK)

**Well Street
Portmahomack
IV20 1YD**

NH 917 846

Church of Scotland

Linked with Fearn Abbey (73)

Off Main Street

Simple rectangular former United Free Church building, architects Andrew Maitland & Sons, 1908. Tarbat Discovery Centre (former Tarbat Old Parish Church) has displays of church and archaeology, including Pictish stones, and a place for private prayer in the crypt. Adjacent archaeological dig ongoing.

- Sunday: 10.00am
- Please ask for key at village shop (50 metres), shop hours only (01862 832626)

84 ROSEMARKIE PARISH CHURCH

**Rosemarkie
IV10 8UF**

NH 737 576

Church of Scotland

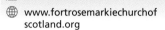
www.fortrosemarkiechurchof scotland.org

Linked with Avoch (67), Fortrose (74)

Off the High Street (A832)

Completed 1821, overlooking the Moray Firth. Rectangular with tall windows and a pinnacled square tower at the west end. Pitch-pine interior with galleries of 1894 by John Robertson; the pulpit incorporates the 1821 crown-shaped canopy. The congregation united with Fortrose in 1967, and services alternate between the two church buildings.

- Sunday: 11.30am in February, April, June, August, October and December, 6.00pm in other months
- Open by arrangement (01381 620381)

85 FODDERTY & STRATHPEFFER PARISH CHURCH

Main Road
Strathpeffer
IV14 9DL

NH 482 580

Church of Scotland

www.strathpefferchurchof
scotland.org

Grey stone church with flèche, designed by William C. Joass and built 1888–90 as part of the development of Strathpeffer as Britain's most northerly spa. A rectangular building with side aisles and balcony to the rear; the chancel extends from the nave under a low roof.

- Sunday: 11.00am; also last Sunday of the month, April to October, 8.00pm
- Open by arrangement (01997 421398)

86 ST ANNE'S CHURCH, STRATHPEFFER

Main Road
Strathpeffer
IV14 9DW

NH 483 580

Scottish Episcopal

www.stjames-stannes.org.uk

Linked with St James's, Dingwall (71)

Cream stone church with round tower. Designed by John Robertson as a memorial to Anne, Duchess of Sutherland and Countess of Cromartie, it was constructed between 1890 and 1892, with the chancel added in 1899. The pulpit is of Caen stone and alabaster, the altar and reredos of marble and alabaster showing carved reliefs. Stained-glass windows are by J. Powell & Sons, 1891, and Heaton, Butler & Bayne, 1892–c. 1910.

- Sunday: 9.30am or 11.00am, alternating with St James's, Dingwall
- Open daily, Easter to September (01349 862204)

87 ST ANDREW'S, TAIN

**Manse Street
Tain
IV19 1HE**

🅰 NH 777 822

🅰 Scottish Episcopal

🌐 www.standrewstain.co.uk/

Designed 1887 by Ross & MacBeth, replacing an earlier corrugated-iron structure. The earliest stained glass, by Ballantine & Gardiner, was moved from the earlier church. Other glass by A. L. Ward, 1910, and W. Wilson, 1955 and 1961. Fine organ by Hamilton & Muller, restored 1986. Forward altar designed and carved from American oak by Peter Bailey of Skye, 1995.

- 1st and 3rd Sunday of the month: 11.15am, 2nd and 4th Sunday: 9.30am, 5th Sunday: as advertised; Thursday: 6.00pm
- Open daily 10.00am–4.00pm (01862 892193)

88 CAWDOR PARISH CHURCH

**Cawdor
IV12 5XP**

🅰 NH 844 499

🅰 Church of Scotland

🌐 www.cawdorparishchurch.co.uk

Linked with Croy & Dalcross (89)

On main road through village (B9090)

Parts of the former church of 1619, including the porch, are incorporated into the present church, which dates from 1830. Cross-shaped with crow-stepped gables and a tower rising from the south gable. The pitch-pine interior was fitted in 1904.

- Sunday: 10.15am
- Open some weekdays during July, August and September; or by arrangement (01667 493217)

Gaelic

89 CROY & DALCROSS PARISH CHURCH

**Croy
IV2 5PH**

 NH 797 499

Church of Scotland

Linked with Cawdor (88)

On B9006, 10km (6 miles) north-east of Culloden Moor

Long, harled, rectangular church built 1764 with a ball finial on the east gable and a birdcage bellcote on the west gable. Pointed arched windows on the south wall provide light to the interior. Handsome table tombs and monuments in the graveyard.

- Sunday: 12.00 noon
- Open by arrangement (01667 493217)

  (in halls)

Gaelic

90 NAIRN OLD PARISH CHURCH

**Academy Street
Nairn
IV12 4RN**

NH 879 564

Church of Scotland

Junction with Inverness Road

Considered the finest structure in the area, 1895–7 by John Starforth. Architecture of Early English Transition period; Gothic reminiscences are abundant. Transeptal in form but almost circular in shape. Square tower is almost 30 metres (100 feet) high. Lovely light interior. Glorious stained glass by Ballantine & Gardiner and Douglas Strachan.

- Sunday: 10.30am
- Open weekdays 9.30am–12.30pm (01667 452382)

 (by arrangement)

91 ST MARY'S CHURCH, BEAULY

**High Street
Beauly
IV4 7AU**

Ⓐ NH 528 467

 Roman Catholic

Linked with Our Lady, Marydale (80), St Mary's, Eskadale (95)

Nave, chancel and north aisle, and adjoining house, built as a unit in red sandstone, 1864, probably by Joseph A. Hansom. Nearby, the ruins of Beauly Priory, founded for Valliscaulian monks in 1230, maintained by Historic Scotland.

- Sunday: Mass 11.00am
- Open by arrangement (01463 782232)

92 DALAROSSIE CHURCH

**Dalarossie
IV13 7YA**

Ⓐ NH 767 242

 Church of Scotland

 www.strathsnairnanddearn.co.uk

Linked with Daviot (93), Dunlichity (94), Moy (108), Tomatin (109)

5km (3 miles) from Tomatin up Strathdearn

Dalarossie Church, on the River Findhorn, is an ancient place of worship dating back to the 8th century at the time of St Fergus. The present building, set within the walled graveyard, dates from 1790 and is a simple whitewashed rectangular church. Features include an ancient baptismal font and a 'covenant stone'.

- April to October: 10.30am on 1st and 3rd Sunday of the month; November to March: 10.30am, 1st Sunday
- Open by arrangement (01463 772242)

Ⓑ 👤 (by arrangement)

HIGHLAND

INVERNESS-SHIRE

93 DAVIOT CHURCH

**Daviot
IV1 2XQ**

🏛 NH 722 394

⛪ Church of Scotland

🌐 www.strathsnairnanddearn.co.uk

Linked with Dalarossie (92), Dunlichity (94), Moy (108), Tomatin (109)

On A9, 10km (6 miles) south of Inverness

The present church dates from 1826 and is situated beside a small hillock, locally known as Cnoc an t-Sagairt, the 'Priest's Hillock'. Restored 1991. There has been a place of worship on the site since early times, long before its charter was granted in the 13th century. The surrounding graveyard tells of the changing history of this interesting parish.

- Sunday: 12.00 noon
- Open by arrangement (01463 772242)

94 DUNLICHITY CHURCH

**Dunlichity
IV1 2AN**

🏛 NH 659 331

⛪ Church of Scotland

🌐 www.strathsnairnanddearn.co.uk

Linked with Dalarossie (92), Daviot (93), Moy (108), Tomatin (109)

Near Loch Duntelchaig

An ancient place of worship, much earlier than the present building, which dates back in part to the 16th century. Many interesting features, including a 1702 handbell, and surrounded by a graveyard of much historical interest, with its own 1759 watch-house.

- May to October: 1st Sunday of the month, 6.30pm
- Open by arrangement (01463 772242)

 (by arrangement)

95 ST MARY'S CHURCH, ESKADALE

**Eskadale
IV4 7JR**

🏹 NH 453 399

⛪ Roman Catholic

Linked with Our Lady, Marydale (80), St Mary's, Beauly (91)

On a minor road on south-east side of River Beauly

A spacious white-harled church in a picturesque woodland setting. Completed 1826 by the 14th Lord Lovat. Alterations and additions by Peter Paul Pugin, 1881. Founder's tomb in the chancel. Lovat family graveyard to the west of the church. The contemporary stable to accommodate horses ridden by those attending Mass, 50 metres to the west of the church, is an unusual feature.

- 9.00am alternate Sundays
- Open by arrangement (01463 782232)

96 FORT AUGUSTUS PARISH CHURCH

**Fort William Road
Fort Augustus
PH32 4BH**

🏹 NH 377 090

⛪ Church of Scotland

🌐 www.cofslochaber.co.uk

Linked with Glengarry (120), Tomdoun (129)

Adjacent to Lovat Arms Hotel Rectangular church with lancet windows and iron bellcote. Reconstruction by Henry Burrell, 1866–7, replacing an earlier church built by public subscription in 1767. Interior recast in 1960. Set in quiet grounds with access from Caledonian Canal side.

- Sunday: 10.00am or 12.00 noon
- Open daily (01320 366210)

HIGHLAND

INVERNESS-SHIRE

97 FORT GEORGE CHAPEL

**Fort George
Ardersier
IV1 2TD**

🏛 NH 761 567

⛪ Non-denominational

🌐 www.historic-scotland.gov.uk

Off A96 north-east of Inverness

Garrison chapel built in 1767, probably to a design by William Skinner. Interior, two-tiered arcade on three sides supported by Roman Doric columns. 18th-century three-decker pulpit. Within working garrison. Visitor displays, Historic Scotland.

- See website
- Open April to September, daily 9.30am–5.30pm; October to March, daily 9.30am–4.30pm (01662 462777)

98 OLD HIGH CHURCH, INVERNESS

**Church Street
Inverness
IV1 1EY**

🏛 NH 665 455

⛪ Church of Scotland

🌐 www.oldhighststephens.com

Linked with St Stephen's, Inverness (106)

Present building completed 1772 to a plan by George Fraser of Edinburgh on site of medieval church; lowest portion of west bell-tower is 15th- or 16th-century. Porches, apse and chancel arch date from 1891, to designs by Ross & Macbeth. Colours and Books of Remembrance of the Queen's Own Cameron Highlanders. 2-manual organ by Henry Willis & Sons, 1895, restored by Nicholson & Co., 2010. Stained glass by, among others, Douglas Strachan, 1925, Stephen Adam & Co., 1893, and A. Ballantine & Gardiner, 1899.

- Sunday: 11.15am; summer evening services as advertised
- Open by arrangement (01463 250802)

99 ST ANDREW'S CATHEDRAL, INVERNESS

**Ardross Street
Inverness
IV3 5NS**

NH 664 449

Scottish Episcopal

www.invernesscathedral.com

On west bank of River Ness, just above Ness Bridge

One of the first new cathedrals completed (1869) in Great Britain after the Reformation; designed by local architect Alexander Ross. In Decorated Gothic style, the building has glorious details including polished granite pillars, encaustic tiles and fine furnishings. Angel font after Thorvaldsen. Stained glass by John Hardman. Founder's memorial, icons presented by Tsar of Russia.

- Sunday: 8.15am, 9.15am, 11.00am and 5.30pm; Matins, Eucharist and Evensong daily
- Open daily 6.00am–5.15pm (01463 233535)

    (May to September 10.30am–3.30pm)

100 ST MARY'S CHURCH, INVERNESS

**30 Huntly Street
Inverness
IV3 5PR**

NH 662 455

Roman Catholic

www.stmarysinverness.co.uk/

On west bank of River Ness

Completed in 1837 by William Robertson in Gothic Revival manner, extended and given a new altar and reredos with carved figures and mosaics by W. L. Carruthers in 1893. Redecorated and new stained-glass window installed to mark the Millennium and the Great Year of Jubilee.

- Saturday: 6.30pm; Sunday: 11.00am and 6.30pm, Polish Mass 1.00pm
- Open daily, summer 9.00am–6.00pm, winter 9.00am–3.00pm (01463 233519)

101 ST MICHAEL & ALL ANGELS, INVERNESS

**Abban Street
Inverness
IV3 8HH**

NH 659 457

Scottish Episcopal

www.angelforce.co.uk/stmichael

Junction with Lochalsh Road

St Michael & All Angels is a church firmly rooted within the Anglo-Catholic Anglican tradition. The 1886 church built on the banks of the River Ness was moved stone by stone and rebuilt in Abban Street in 1903–4 under the guidance of architect Alexander Ross. 1924 alterations by Sir Ninian Comper, making it 'the Comper Jewel in the Highlands'. The font with its lofty steeple cover is also by Comper in memory of his father, Rev. John Comper. Open every day of the week … so come and visit us!

- Sunday: 11.00am; check website for full list of other services
- Open daily 10.00am–6.00pm and by arrangement (01463 233797)

 (by arrangement)  (by arrangement)

102 CROWN CHURCH, INVERNESS

**Kingsmill Road
Inverness
IV2 3JT**

NH 671 452

Church of Scotland

http://crown-church.co.uk

Junction with Midmills Road

Designed by J. R. Rhind and completed in 1901, though without intended spire and with subsequent extensions to the halls. Stained glass in rose and west windows. Organ 3-manual by Makin. Centenary wall hanging.

- Sunday: 11.00am and 6.30pm, in summer also 9.30am; prayers weekdays 12.00 noon
- Open daily, mornings in winter, all day in summer (01463 231140)

103 **INVERNESS FREE NORTH CHURCH**

Bank Street
Inverness
IV1 1QU

⚑ NH 665 455

⛪ Free Church of Scotland

🌐 www.freenorthchurch.org

Gothic church designed by Alexander Ross and completed 1893. Seating capacity is 1,500, making it the largest church in Inverness; it also has the tallest steeple. The internal woodwork is a special feature. The church has recently been extensively renovated and redecorated in the original colours.

- Sunday: 11.00am and 6.30pm; Wednesday: 7.30pm
- Open by arrangement (01463 790220)

Gaelic

 104 **INVERNESS METHODIST CHURCH**

50 Huntly Street
Inverness
IV3 5HS

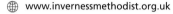

⚑ NH 663 455

⛪ Methodist

🌐 www.invernessmethodist.org.uk

The present building was built 1964–5 to replace one destroyed by fire; architect Kenneth Finlayson of John R. Chisholm & Co. A new entrance and floodlighting were provided in 2003. Wood pews with ash stringing to provide contrast. Six main windows have stained glass; one commemorates the visit of John Wesley to Inverness in 1764. Organ by Rushworth & Dreaper, 1965.

- Sunday: 11.00am all year, 5.00pm November to March, 6.00pm April to October; Wednesday: 12.15pm
- Open by arrangement (01463 231170)

105 NESS BANK CHURCH, INVERNESS

**Ness Bank
Inverness
IV2 4SF**

NH 666 448

Church of Scotland

www.nessbank.com

At Haugh Road

The church, which seats 700, was completed in 1901 on a steeply sloping site with the hall and other accommodation under the church. Designed by William Mackintosh in early Gothic Revival style in red sandstone with freestone dressings. Stained glass by Gordon Webster, St Enoch Studios, Isobel Goudie and William Wilson. Organ James F. Binns, 1903, altered by Rushworth & Dreaper, 1980.

- Sunday: 11.00am September to June, 10.00am July and August; occasional evening services
- Open by arrangement (01463 234653)

 106 ST STEPHEN'S, INVERNESS

**Southside Road
Inverness
IV2 3AU**

NH 672 449

Church of Scotland

www.oldhighststephens.com

Linked with Old High Church, Inverness (98)

Junction with Edinburgh Road

By W. L. Carruthers, 1897, in Arts & Crafts Gothic, the hall added later. The church consists of a nave, single north transept and an apsidal chancel. Square tower with a delicate needle spire. High open roof, pulpit of locally grown native oak. Noteworthy stained glass of 1897 and 1906 by A. Ballantine & Son. 2-manual organ by Wadsworth Bros, 1902, substantially renovated in 2000 by Sandy Edmonstone.

- Sunday: 10.00am, evenings as advertised
- Open by arrangement (01463 250802)

107 TWEEDMOUTH MEMORIAL CHAPEL, INVERNESS

Royal Northern Infirmary
Ness Walk
Inverness
IV3 5SS

NH 663 445

Inter-denominational

Earliest example of purpose-built ecumenical worship space in Scotland, completed in 1898, architects A. Ross and R. B. MacBeth. Three sanctuary areas for Reformed, Roman Catholic and Episcopalian worship.

- Occasional services
- Keys available from hospital porters (01463 704463)

108 MOY CHURCH

Moy
IV3 7YE

NH 772 342

Church of Scotland

www.strathsnairnanddearn.co.uk

Linked with Dalarossie (92), Daviot (93), Dunlichity (94), Tomatin (109)

On old A9, 16km (10 miles) south-east of Inverness

Built in 1765, on a previous site, and surrounded by an interesting graveyard with its own watch-house. Memorial stone to Donald Fraser, the hero of the 'Rout of Moy', just before the Battle of Culloden in 1746.

- 10.30am, 4th Sunday of the month, April to October; 3rd and 5th Sunday, November to March
- Open by arrangement (01463 772242)

  (by arrangement)

109 TOMATIN CHURCH

**Tomatin
IV13 7YR**

NH 803 290

Church of Scotland

www.strathsnairnanddearn.co.uk

Linked with Dalarossie (92), Daviot (93), Dunlichity (94), Moy (108)

On east side of old A9 in village of Tomatin

A fine example of the 'tin churches' erected c. 1910 by the United Free Church to serve as mission churches and halls in areas of new population. Remarkably complete timber-lined interior.

- 10.30am, 2nd and 5th Sunday of the month, April to October; 10.30am, 2nd and 4th Sunday, November to March
- Open by arrangement (01463 772242)

 (by arrangement)

110 ST ANDREW'S, AVIEMORE

**Main Street
Aviemore
PH22 1RL**

NH 895 131

Church of Scotland

Neat Gothic church in granite by James Gilbert, 1899–1901. War memorial carved by class of Gertrude Martineau.

- Sunday: 11.15am
- Open by arrangement (01479 810280)

111 ST COLUMBA'S, GRANTOWN-ON-SPEY

**High Street
Grantown-on-Spey
PH26 3EL**

⚔ NJ 029 274

⛪ Scottish Episcopal

🌐 www.morayrossandcaithness.co.uk

Near Craiglynne Hotel

Small rectangular granite-built church with a flèche by Ross & Macbeth, 1892–3. Noteworthy stained glass, c. 1900, including a window above the organ to St Cecilia. The small but welcoming congregation celebrated its centenary in 2005 and built the small adjacent hall the same year. The building also hosts Roman Catholic services.

- Sunday: Episcopal 10.30am; Roman Catholic 4.15pm
- Open by arrangement (01479 872255)

112 KINGUSSIE PARISH CHURCH

**High Street
Kingussie
PH21 1HY**

⚔ NH 762 007

⛪ Church of Scotland

A 'Columban' church, thought to have been a place of worship since the 11th century. The present building of 1792, set back within its churchyard, was refurbished after a fire in 1924. Features a pitch-pine roof, Arts & Crafts stained-glass windows and carvings by pupils of the Misses Martineau from London.

- Sunday: 11.00am
- Open by arrangement (01540 661311)

113 ST JOHN THE BAPTIST, ROTHIEMURCHUS

Inverdruie
PH22 1QH

⚔ NH 900 111

⛪ Scottish Episcopal

🌐 www.stjohn-rothiemurchus.co.uk

B970, 1.6km (1 mile) east of Aviemore

'The little white church on the ski road.' Church founded by John Peter Grant, 11th Laird of Rothiemurchus, and consecrated in 1931. Architect Sir Ninian Comper. A plain white interior with a groin-vaulted ceiling and a rose damask baldacchino. Simple burial ground surrounds the church.

- Sunday: 10.30am
- Open by arrangement (01540 661875)

 114 ARDGOUR CHURCH

North Corran
Ardgour
PH33 7AA

⚔ NN 011 642

⛪ Church of Scotland

🌐 www.rockofpeace.co.uk/church/

Linked with Kingairloch (121), Morvern (Lochaline) (124), Strontian (128)

1.6km (1 mile) north of Corran Ferry

Parliamentary church designed by William Thompson, 1829, with Tudor windows and pinnacled bellcote. In 1993, a new vestibule, meeting room, vestry, kitchen and toilet were added.

- Sunday service alternates with Strontian: 10.00am in even-numbered years, 11.45am in odd-numbered years
- Open daily (01855 841367)

115 GLENCOE ST MUNDA'S CHURCH, BALLACHULISH

Ballachulish
PH49 4JG

NN 083 578

Church of Scotland

www.argyllandtheisles.org.uk/
glencoe.html

Linked with Duror (117)

On right bank of River Laroch in centre of Ballachulish

The original church of St Munda was on Eilean Munda, an island in Loch Leven. Traditional church of 1845 with battlemented tower added 1881. Banners, made by church members, tell of Ballachulish life.

- Sunday: 11.00am
- Open from dawn to dusk (01855 811998)

116 ST MUN'S CHURCH, BALLACHULISH

Brecklet
Ballachulish
PH49 4LG

NN 083 579

Roman Catholic

South side of village, off A82

Built 1836 by Bishop Scott, Vicar-Apostolic for the West of Scotland. Simple Highland church in good condition. Adjacent building was originally the priest's house.

- Sunday: 11.00am; daily as announced
- Open daily (01855 811203)

117 DUROR PARISH CHURCH

**Duror
PA38 4DA**

- NM 994 554
- Church of Scotland
- www.argyllandtheisles.org.uk/
  duror.html

Linked with Glencoe (115)

On A828, 8km (5 miles) from
Ballachulish

A traditional Thomas Telford church,
completed 1827. Built of rubble stone
with slate roof and pyramid-topped
bellcote. Inside, the furnishings are
Victorian.

- Sunday: 9.30am
- Open from dawn to dusk
  (01855 811998)

 (Wednesday mornings,
July and August)

118 ST MARY'S,
FORT WILLIAM

**Belford Road
Fort William
PH33 6BT**

- NN 107 741
- Roman Catholic

Across A82 from railway station

Designed by Reginald Fairlie and built
1933–4. The nave is a plain box of grey
granite with round-arched windows
with a tower of pink and grey granite.
Inside, a simple barrel-vaulted nave
with oak pews. Lady Chapel with oak
reredos. The chancel has a wrought-
iron baldacchino by Thomas Bogie.
Organ by Sniffen & Stroud.

- Saturday: 7.00pm; Sunday: 9.00am,
  11.00am and 4.00pm; Monday to
  Saturday: 10.15am
- Open daily 9.00am–6.30pm
  (01397 702174)

Gaelic

119 ST MARY AND ST FINNAN, GLENFINNAN

Glenfinnan
PH37 4LT

NM 904 808

Roman Catholic

In village, on A830

Consecrated in 1873, the church, designed by E. Welby Pugin in the Gothic style, enjoys an elevated and commanding position overlooking Loch Shiel. Spectacular views of the loch and surrounding hills. The church is a memorial chapel to the MacDonalds of Glenaladale, the family with whom Bonnie Prince Charlie stayed prior to the raising of the Jacobite standard at Glenfinnan in August 1745.

- Sunday: 1.00pm
- Open daily, sunrise to sunset (01397 722251)

120 GLENGARRY PARISH CHURCH

Invergarry
PH35 4HL

NH 304 012

Church of Scotland

www.cofslochaber.co.uk

Linked with Fort Augustus (96), Tomdoun (129)

West of Invergarry Hotel on A87

Charming simple Gothic church built under the patronage of the Ellice family of Glengarry. Grey granite with red sandstone dressings by Alexander Ross, 1864–5; chancel, transepts and tower added 1896–7. Organ by Ingram & Co., 1898, rebuilt and relocated within the church by George Sixsmith, 1985.

- Sunday: 10.00am or 12.00 noon
- Open daily May to October (01320 366210)

HIGHLAND

LOCHABER

121 ## KINGAIRLOCH CHURCH

**Camus-na-Croise
Kingairloch
PH33 7AE**

NM 862 526

Church of Scotland

www.rockofpeace.co.uk/church/

Linked with Ardgour (114), Morvern (Lochaline) (124), Strontian (128)

On B8043

White-harled stone church overlooking Loch Linnhe, with red eaves and doors in estate style, on land gifted by the Forbes family in 1857. Belfry erected 1897 by George Sherriff in memory of his father John Bell Sherriff. Stained glass by A. Ballantine & Son, 1906.

• Sunday: 3.00pm on 2nd Sunday of the month all year, and 2nd and 4th Sunday Easter to end October
• Open daily (01595 859517)

 122 ## KINLOCHLEVEN PARISH CHURCH

**Riverside Road
Kinlochleven
PH50 4QW**

NN 187 621

Church of Scotland

www.netherlochaberchurch.co.uk/

Linked with Onich (127)

Off A82

Built 1930 to a simple but elegant design by J. Jeffrey Waddell, with a high arch at the chancel end. Chancel area is a round bell-shape with stained-glass windows depicting biblical scenes. Two stained-glass windows in the south wall of the nave depict St Andrew and St George.

• Sunday: 10.00am; also 6.30pm, 2nd and 4th Sunday of the month
• Open by arrangement (01855 831765)

123 ST FINAN'S CHURCH, KINLOCHMOIDART

Kinlochmoidart
PH38 4ND

△ NM 710 728

♨ Scottish Episcopal

Up a track leading off the A861, 800 metres (½ mile) north of bridge over River Moidart

The church stands in woodland above the mouth of the River Moidart and below an impressively steep hillside. It was built in 1857–60 to a design by Alexander Ross in simple Early English style, with crow-stepped gables, a small belfry and a porch. Two stained-glass windows by the Victorian artist Jemima Blackburn.

- 5.30pm, 1st Sunday of the month
- Open daily (01967 431225)

 124 MORVERN PARISH CHURCH, LOCHALINE

Kiel Parish Church

Lochaline
PA34 5XU

△ NM 672 452

♨ Church of Scotland

⊕ www.rockofpeace.co.uk/church/

Linked with Ardgour (114), Kingairloch (121), Strontian (128)

1.6km (1 mile) out of Lochaline on the Drimnin road

The original church, according to legend, was erected at the command of St Columba. Today's church was designed by Peter Macgregor Chalmers in 1898. Interesting stained glass. Memorial plaque to the MacLeods, father and son, whose ministry here spanned more than a century. 15th-century cross outside the front of the church. Collection of 8th- to 16th-century carved stones in 18th-century session house.

- Sunday: 11.00am
- Open daily (01967 421208)

HIGHLAND

LOCHABER

125 ST PATRICK'S, MALLAIG

Mallaig
PH41 4RF

NM 675 968

Roman Catholic

Linked with Our Lady, Morar (126)

On A830

Canon John MacNeill came from Morar to say Mass in the school until 1935, when the church, designed by Reginald Fairley, was opened. The open-timbered roof, similar to that at Morar, is a feature. The stained-glass windows were first in the 'tin' (or iron) Cathedral at Oban, paid for by the Marquess of Bute.

• Sunday: 10.00am; Monday, Wednesday and Friday: 10.00am
• Open 9.00am–8.00pm (01687 462201)

126 OUR LADY OF PERPETUAL SUCCOUR & ST CUMIN, MORAR

Morar
PH40 4PB

NM 686 928

Roman Catholic

Linked with St Patrick's, Mallaig (125)

At west end of Loch Morar, 800 metres (½ mile) from Morar railway station

Built and dedicated by the Lovat family in 1889 for the people of the area. Overlooking the lovely Loch Morar, it is built of local grey stone with a detached bell-tower. Inside are interesting stained-glass windows, including a recent one above the choir loft depicting the life of St Cumin.

• Sunday: 11.30am; Tuesday and Saturday: 10.00am; Thursday: 6.00pm
• Open 9.00am–8.00pm (01687 462201)

127 NETHER LOCHABER PARISH CHURCH, ONICH

Onich
PH33 6SD

A NN 031 614

Church of Scotland

www.netherlochaberchurch.co.uk/

Linked with Kinlochleven (122)

18km (11 miles) south of Fort William on A82

Built in 1911 to replace original Telford church at Creag Mhor, using some of the original stone. Known as one of the finest rural churches in the Highlands. Most illustrious minister was Dr Alexander Stewart, 1851–1901, known as 'Nether Lochaber' and renowned throughout the Celtic world for his wide-ranging learning and writing.

- Sunday: 12.00 noon
- Open by arrangement (01855 821003)

128 STRONTIAN CHURCH

Strontian
PH36 4JB

A NM 815 625

Church of Scotland

www.rockofpeace.co.uk/church/

Linked with Ardgour (114), Kingairloch (121), Morvern (Lochaline) (124)

800 metres (½ mile) up road to Polloch from main coast road

Parliamentary church built to the standard 'Telford' design of William Thomson, completed 1829. Remodelled 1924. Granite walls with sandstone margins and slate roof.

- Sunday service alternates with Ardgour: 10.00am in odd-numbered years, 11.45am in even-numbered years
- Open daily (01687 402409)

129 TOMDOUN CHURCH

**Tomdoun
PH35 4HS**

NH 155 012
Church of Scotland
www.cofslochaber.co.uk

Linked with Fort Augustus (96),
Glengarry (120)

On road to Kinlochhourn, west of
Tomdoun Hotel

Built by Glengarry Estate to serve
upper Glengarry. Simple T-plan
church in stone with slate roof. Its
peace and its setting are much valued
by visitors.

- 3.00pm, 2nd Sunday of the month
- Open daily (01320 366210)

**130 BROADFORD PARISH
CHURCH, SKYE**

**Broadford
Isle of Skye
IV49 9AB**

NG 643 235
Church of Scotland
www.sschurch.co.uk

Linked with Elgol (131), Kilmore
(132), Kyleakin (133)

Opposite main car park

Typical small rectangular church of
1839–41 with round-headed windows
and pedimented bellcote. Window
glazing altered 1880s, and interior
altered 1930s.

- Sunday: 10.15am, and 6.00pm on
  last Sunday of the month
- Open by arrangement (01471 820063)

Gaelic

131 ELGOL PARISH CHURCH, SKYE

Elgol
Isle of Skye
IV49 9BL

 NG 523 143

Church of Scotland

www.sschurch.co.uk

Linked with Broadford (130), Kilmore (132), Kyleakin (133)

B8083, before steep descent to Elgol pier

Iron-clad structure of 1898 with stunning views across Loch Scavaig to the Cuillin hills. Recently renovated with new windows and refurbished interior and furnishings. An attractive and appealing place of worship.

- Sunday: 6.00pm on 1st and 3rd Sunday of the month
- Open by arrangement (01471 820063)

Gaelic

132 KILMORE PARISH CHURCH, SKYE

Kilmore
Isle of Skye
IV44 8RG

 NG 657 069

Church of Scotland

www.sschurch.co.uk

Linked with Broadford (130), Elgol (131), Kyleakin (133)

A851, 5km (3 miles) north-east of Armadale

A' Chill Mhor, 'the great cell', refers to the old church, now a ruin beside the present church, a large rectangular whitewashed building with lancet windows designed by John Mackenzie and built 1876–7. The Victorian furnishings are complete. Notable monuments flank the pulpit, including one of 1768 to Sir James Macdonald. Close by is Sabhal Mòr Ostaig, a steading of 1840 converted into a Gaelic college.

- Sunday: 11.00am
- Open by arrangement (01471 820063)

Gaelic

HIGHLAND

SKYE & LOCHALSH

KYLEAKIN PARISH CHURCH, SKYE

**Kyleakin
Isle of Skye
IV41 8PH**

NG 751 263

Church of Scotland

www.sschurch.co.uk

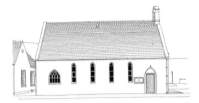

Linked with Broadford (130), Elgol (131), Kilmore (132)

Adjacent to King's Arms Hotel

Small whitewashed church with lancet windows, built 1875. Heated and lit by paraffin lamps until 1947, when electricity came to Kyleakin, and the Women's Guild raised funds for the church heating system.

- Sunday: 12.00 noon and 6.00pm (except last Sunday of the month)
- Open by arrangement (01471 820063)

PORTREE PARISH CHURCH, SKYE

**Somerled Square
Portree
Isle of Skye
IV51 9EH**

NG 482 436

Church of Scotland

St Columba brought Christianity to Skye, and the ruins of earlier churches are to be seen in and around Portree. The present building, designed by John Hay of Liverpool, was built as a Free Church in 1854, becoming United Free Church in 1900 and Church of Scotland in 1929. Stained-glass windows by Douglas Hamilton and Thomas Webster.

- Sunday: 11.00am and 6.30pm
- Open throughout the summer, 11.00am–4.00pm

Gaelic

135 ST COLUMBA'S, PORTREE

**Park Road
Portree
Isle of Skye
IV51 9EH**

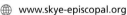

NG 482 437

Scottish Episcopal

www.skye-episcopal.org

Off Somerled Square

Elizabethan-style church with
continuous nave and chancel, 1884,
by Alexander Ross. Stained-glass
window of Queen Esther, a memorial
to Flora Macdonald by E. I. Ingram,
and some tapestries.

- Sunday: 11.00am; also in
  Community Centre on Raasay
  at 2.00pm on 2nd Monday of the
  month, and at Sabhal Mòr Ostaig,
  Old Campus, Sleat at 6.00pm on 2nd
  Sunday of the month
- Open daily during the summer

136 ST MOLUAG, EOROPAIDH, LEWIS

Eoropaidh
Ness
Lewis
HS2 0XA

NB 519 651

Scottish Episcopal

www.saintmoluag.com

Linked with St Moluag's, Tong (139)

200 metres from B8013 (signposted Eoropaidh from A857)

The building probably dates from the 13th century, but the site is believed to have been consecrated in the 6th century and is probably the place where Christianity was first preached to the people of Lewis. Restored in 1912 by Norman Forbes of Stornoway, architect J. S. Richardson. The church has no heating, electricity or water; lighting is by candles and oil lamps. No vehicular access. In wet weather, path to church can be muddy.

- May to September: 11.00am, 1st Sunday of the month; 3.00pm, 3rd Sunday of the month
- Open during daylight hours (01851 820657)

137 ST COLUMBA'S (OLD PARISH) CHURCH, STORNOWAY, LEWIS

Lewis Street
Stornoway
Lewis
HS1 2JF

NB 426 330

Church of Scotland

Successor to St Lennan's Church Stornoway and St Columba's Uidh, the church of 1794 by John Lobban, master mason, was repaired in 1831 and extended in 1885. Caen stone and marble font gifted by Lady Matheson of the Lews. 2-manual pipe organ, Joseph Brook; rebuilt 1954, Henry Willis & Co. Oak sanctuary furniture and brass eagle lectern gifted by Greyfriars Tolbooth and Highland Kirk, Edinburgh.

- Sunday: 11.00am and 6.30pm; Thursday: 7.30pm
- Open by arrangement (01851 706521)

Gaelic

WESTERN ISLES

138 OUR HOLY REDEEMER CHURCH, STORNOWAY, LEWIS

Scotland Street
Stornoway
Lewis
HS1 2DS

NB 425 329

Roman Catholic

Corner of Kenneth Street

Much local material – Lewisian gneiss, Borve pottery, Harris tweed – is used in this white-harled cruciform church, built 2005–7. Tapestry of Our Holy Redeemer by Meg Thompson. Antique oak crucifix donated by the Diocese of Aachen, Germany. Custom-made oak lectern, presidential chair and curved ash pews. Antique brass-domed tabernacle, Italian woodcarvings of Christ, Virgin and Child and of Stations of the Cross.

- Saturday: 6.00pm; Sunday: 11.00am; weekdays as announced
- Open weekdays 8.00am–7.00pm, Sunday 10.30am–7.30pm (01851 702070)

Gaelic

139 ST MOLUAG'S COMMUNITY CHURCH, TONG, LEWIS

Tong
Lewis
HS2 0HY

NB 449 366

Scottish Episcopal

www.saintmoluag.com

Linked with St Moluag's, Eoropaidh (136)

Opposite Tong School, on B895

The historic 12th-century St Moluag's, Eoropaidh, has no heating, lighting or water, so in 2000 the former Tong village shop and post office was converted into an attractive, modern, multi-purpose church. The building is also available for community use when there are no services. Interest in the old church at Eoropaidh is truly international, and our visitors throughout the summer months include people from all over the world.

- Sunday: 11.00am (except 1st Sunday of the month from May to September, and Easter Day – service at Eoropaidh)
- Open by arrangement (01851 820657 or 01851 704540)

140 ST CLEMENT'S CHURCH, RODEL, HARRIS

**Rodel
Harris
HS5 3TW**

 NG 047 831

Non-denominational

www.historic-scotland.gov.uk

On A859 in village

A fine 16th-century church built by Alexander MacLeod of Dunvegan and Harris; his richly carved tomb is within the church. St Clement was the third Bishop of Rome after St Peter and was martyred in AD 99. The church is in the care of Historic Scotland.

- Services by arrangement
- Open dawn to dusk all year
  (01667 460202)

141 BERNERAY CHURCH

**Borgh
Berneray
HS6 5BB**

 NF 920 818

Church of Scotland

Built 1887, architect Thomas Binnie of Glasgow, for the United Free Church. By uniting with the Established Church, whose building is now in ruins, it became the Church of Scotland and still flourishes as such. HRH the Prince of Wales worshipped here on a private visit in 1991. Berneray is now accessible by a causeway from North Uist across the Sound of Harris.

- Sunday: 12.00 noon or 6.00pm, alternating with Lochmaddy
- Open by arrangement (01876 500414)

Gaelic

KILMUIR CHURCH, NORTH UIST

**Balranald
North Uist
HS6 5DW**

A NF 727 703

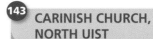 Church of Scotland

On A865

Originally North Uist Parish Church. Gothic T-plan by Alexander Sharp, 1892–4. In the south-west inner angle is a two-stage tower, its battlemented parapet enclosing a slated pyramidal spire. Inside is a wealth of pitch-pine. One of the few remaining Gaelic-essential charges; during the morning Gaelic service, one can hear, and participate in, the precenting of Gaelic psalms.

- Sunday: 10.00am in Gaelic, 6.00pm in English
- Open by arrangement (01876 510344)

Gaelic

CARINISH CHURCH, NORTH UIST

**Cairinis
North Uist
HS6 5HL**

A NF 820 604

Church of Scotland

Linked with Clachan (144)

On A865

Built as a mission church in 1867 for the Church of Scotland. The main feature is that the communion pews run down the length of the church so that those taking communion would sit side-on to the pulpit. They would be invited to come and sit at the table to take communion.

- No regular services
- Open by arrangement

WESTERN ISLES

 144 CLACHAN CHURCH, NORTH UIST

Clachan na Luib
North Uist
HS6 5HD

NF 811 638

Church of Scotland

Linked with Carinish (143)

On A865

Built 1889 for the Clachan na Luib Free Church, architect Thomas Binnie of Glasgow. Considerable difficulty was experienced procuring the site from Sir William Powlet Campbell Orde, Bart. After lengthy negotiations, he reluctantly gave the present site at an annual rental of £3 9s. The congregation became United Free until 1929, when they became part of the Church of Scotland.

- Sunday: 12.00 noon and 6.00pm in English, unless otherwise announced
- Open by arrangement

145 DALIBURGH CHURCH, SOUTH UIST

Daliburgh
South Uist
HS8 5SS

NF 754 214

Church of Scotland

Linked with Howmore (148)

At junction of A865 and B888

Built originally as South Uist Free Church in 1862–3, now Church of Scotland. Church, hall and manse are all harled. Church rectangular in plan, with three bays with round-headed openings and a single window in either gable. Door and apex belfry to south gable. Pulpit with panelled front. Communion table and war memorial based on design of that at Howmore by Archibald Scott.

- Sunday: 11.00am
- Open daily (01878 700265)

ST PETER'S, DALIBURGH, SOUTH UIST

**Daliburgh
South Uist
HS8 5SS**

NF 745 211

Roman Catholic

Linked with Our Lady, Garrynamonie (147)

1.6km (1 mile) west of junction of A865 and B888

Big harled church of 1868 with a birdcage bellcote on the south gable and a tall concrete hoop bellcote on the 1960s porch. North sanctuary added 1907.

- Sunday: Mass 11.30am
- Open daily (01878 700305)

 ## OUR LADY OF SORROWS, GARRYNAMONIE, SOUTH UIST

**Garrynamonie
South Uist
HS8 5TY**

NF 758 165

Roman Catholic

Linked with St Peter's, Daliburgh (146)

On B888 near south of island

An important Modernist building of 1965 in a spectacular setting. Designed by architect Richard J. McCarron, the simple and massive exterior combined with the carefully lit interior make it an exemplar of its type. Largely self-built by the parishioners; building took 15 months. Stations of the Cross by Canon Calum MacNeill, a local priest. Ceramic of the Sacred Heart by David Harding of Edinburgh. Mural at the entrance by Michael Gilfeddar, 1994.

- Saturday: 6.30pm
- Open daily (01878 700305)

WESTERN ISLES

WESTERN ISLES

 148 HOWMORE CHURCH, SOUTH UIST

**Howmore
South Uist
HS8 5SH**

NF 757 364

Church of Scotland

Linked with Daliburgh (145)

1.6km (1 mile) west of A865

Simple, austere building by John McDearmid, 1858, set in open land overlooking the Atlantic. Acts as landmark for west-coast fishermen. One of the few churches in Scotland with central communion table. Nearby are remains of a 13th-century church.

- Sunday: 11.45am
- Open daily (01870 620314)

149 OUR LADY STAR OF THE SEA, CASTLEBAY, BARRA

**Castlebay
Barra
HS9 5XD**

NL 667 983

Roman Catholic

 www.barracatholic.co.uk

Linked with St Brendan, Craigston (150), Our Lady, Vatersay (154)

Opened Christmas 1886, architect Woulfe Brenan of Oban. Statue by Dupon of Bruges of Our Lady Star of the Sea. Stained glass of crucifixion in sanctuary, and of Our Lady Star of the Sea installed as war memorial in early 1950s. Bell in tower; the clock chimes the hour during day and night.

- Sunday: 11.00am
- Open daily (01871 810267)

**150 ST BRENDAN,
CRAIGSTON, BARRA**

**Craigston
Barra
HS9 5XS**

🗻 NF 657 018

🏛 Roman Catholic

🌐 www.barracatholic.co.uk

**Linked with Our Lady, Castlebay
(149), Our Lady, Vatersay (154)**

Off A888 on west side of island

Dating from 1805, the oldest church
in the Isles of Barra. Simple, harled,
oblong, three-bay church with
pointed windows and a gabled
porch. Restored 1858. Two etchings
(scraperboard white on black) of St
Brendan and St Barr, by Fr Calum
MacNeill, former priest of the diocese.

- Saturday: 7.00pm
- Open daily (01871 810267)

 **151 ST VINCENT DE PAUL,
EOLIGARRY, BARRA**

**Eoligarry
Barra
HS9 5YD**

🗻 NF 703 076

🏛 Roman Catholic

🌐 www.barracatholic.co.uk

**Linked with Cille Bharra (152), St
Barr's (153)**

At north end of island

Built in 1964, the church has a tall
roof with swept eaves. Small cemetery
at Cille Bharra, burial place of MacNeil
chieftains.

- Sunday: 11.00am
- Open daily (01871 890228)

WESTERN ISLES

152 NORTH CHAPEL, CILLE BHARRA

**Cille Bharra
Eoligarry
Barra
HS9 5YE**

NF 705 074

Roman Catholic

www.barracatholic.co.uk

Linked with St Vincent's (151), St Barr's (153)

At north end of island

12th-century church built on site of 7th-century foundation dedicated to St Finbarr of Cork, Eire. Reroofed with help from the Scottish Development Department. Contains notable 12th-century runic stone (original now in the National Museums of Scotland, Edinburgh) and 16th-century grave-slabs with carvings of animals and foliage.

- Mass on the feasts of the Celtic saints
- Open daily (01871 810267)

153 ST BARR'S, NORTHBAY, BARRA

**Northbay
Barra
HS9 5YQ**

NF 707 031

Roman Catholic

www.barracatholic.co.uk

Linked with St Vincent's (151), Cille Bharra (152)

On A888, close to junction with road to Eoligarry

A simple lancet-windowed building by G. Woulfe Brenan, 1906, with porch and vestry added 1919. Small bellcote on porch.

- Sunday: 11.00am; weekdays: 7.30pm
- Open daily (01871 890228)

154 OUR LADY OF THE WAVES & ST JOHN, VATERSAY

**Uidh
Vatersay
HS9 5YW**

Å NL 646 961

🚹 Roman Catholic

⊕ www.barracatholic.co.uk

Linked with Our Lady, Castlebay (149), St Brendan, Craigston (150)

2½km (1½ miles) south of causeway to Barra

Small functional church for celebration of Mass and other church services. Reached by causeway from Barra.

- Sunday: 3.30pm
- Open daily (01871 810267)

155 THE CHURCH, ST KILDA

**Village Bay
St Kilda**

Å NF 104 992

🚹 Inter-denominational

⊕ www.kilda.org.uk

The stimulus for the church, designed by Robert Stevenson for the Free Kirk, came from Rev. Dr John Macdonald, who visited St Kilda several times in the early 19th century. The church fell into disrepair after evacuation in 1930. Renovated over a period of 20 years since coming into the care of the National Trust for Scotland in 1957. St Kilda was Scotland's first World Heritage Site.

- Services by arrangement
- For access, contact the National Trust for Scotland (08444 932100)

WC (nearby)

Index

References are to each church's entry number in the gazetteer.